THE GOAL GETTER

35 DIFFERENT WAYS TO REACH YOUR GOALS

GERRY DUFFY

Ballpoint Press

Published in 2015 by Ballpoint Press
4 Wyndham Park, Bray, Co Wicklow, Republic of Ireland.
Telephone: 00353 86 821 7631
Email: ballpointpress1@gmail.com
Web: www.ballpointpress.ie

ISBN 978-0-9932892-3-1

While every effort has been made to ensure the accuracy of
all information contained in this book, neither the author
nor the publisher accepts liability for any errors or omissions made.

Book design and production by Joe Coyle,
joecoyledesign@gmail.com

Front cover inset photograph:
Gerry Duffy, photographed by Andrew Finnerty

Printed and bound by GraphyCems

CONTENTS

ABOUT THE AUTHOR

GERRY DUFFY (*b. 1968*) is a full-time professional speaker and business trainer. His company, *Gerry Duffy Academy*, helps to inspire and empower professional and personal development.

Gerry's CV is a mixture of sporting endeavour and running his own businesses since 2003. In 2010 along with a friend, Ken Whitelaw, he ran 32 marathons in 32 days (a story outlined in his first book, *Who Dares, Runs*).

A year later Gerry completed and won the inaugural UK DECA-Iron Distance Triathlon, an event dubbed, 'The toughest 10-day endurance challenge in the world'. Competitors were required to swim 24 miles, cycle 1,160 miles and run 262 miles. His second book *Tick, Tock, Ten* chronicles that 10-day ambition and was shortlisted for Irish Sports Book of the Year (2013).

At one time in his life however, Gerry had little ambition and even less motivation. In 1995, he was overweight and a heavy smoker, but he took up running at the age of 27 – and it changed his life. Not only did it improve his physical health, it helped him discover and identify many facets with which he was dissatisfied – fitness, health, career and education.

In a former life, Gerry's greatest fear was public speaking. Since he has overcome it, he has addressed the workforces of companies such as Facebook, Google, Bank of America, Boston Scientific, Norvartis Pharmaceuticals, Forever Living and Coca-Cola.

He lives in Ireland and travels throughout Ireland, Europe and America delivering keynote presentations, workshops and business seminars.

For fun, he runs ultra-marathons.

PREVIOUSLY BY THE SAME AUTHOR

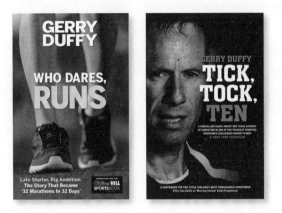

WHO DARES, RUNS
(2011)

TICK, TOCK, TEN
(2013)

Both available in print format or Kindle App
through Amazon or www.gerryduffyacademy.com

ACKNOWLEDGEMENTS

FOR the third time, I am grateful to the following group of people...

To PJ Cunningham, from Ballpoint Press. As ever PJ, a big thank you.

To Joe Coyle from Joe Coyle Design, thank you for your time, patience and your expertise.

To Tom Duffy (Senior) and James Martin for helping me proof the book – a tough job for sure.

And finally to Jacinta O'Neill (my better half). Thank you for your continued support and patience and also for showing me an important signpost just before we went to print.

READ THIS... AND LEAP

THIS is a simple book. It is a series of stories, philosophies, beliefs and strategies that I firmly believe – if acted upon – will not only assist you in progressing your goals, but also, crucially, to get them across the line.

I hope it is a little different to any other book you might have read about achieving goals. That was one of my own goals in writing it. What I can tell you, is that at some point, every message contained in this book has helped me in my life and with my goals. Depending on where you are at any time, you might see something of value to you today or tomorrow, next month or next year.

I must highlight two important things before you read further. The first is that, in so much as is possible, we should chose goals that are aligned with where we want to go. The value of this will become especially apparent when you read Chapter 15, *What's Your 'Why'*. Realise also, that this can and often does change as we journey through life. What will be a priority one year, may be less so at another time.

Secondly – on a number of occasions, I will share a story or philosophy with a sport or exercise theme. Please understand that this is not a sports book. I just happen to believe that exercise is a critical key that can help us in every area of our lives.

Thank you for investing in this book and enjoy the read.

Gerry Duffy

1

THE NUMBER ONE RULE

Bringing respect to every goal

I FIRST opened my own business in 2003, but it's in the running of it and others since, that I've really become educated in life.

One of the earliest lessons I learnt was to have respect for my goals – in this case, business and trade. I realised quite quickly that a business transaction wasn't complete until the payment had hit my bank account – and that it was lodged by a satisfied customer.

My business back then was very different to what I do now. I was in the property business (sales, letting and management) and I had 60 to 80 clients a year. At any time, I might think I had a deal done after shaking hands, but legal work and other issues outside of my control could conspire to delay the process for up to six months. On at least one in five occasions – and for no reason in particular – the deal would fall through.

I learned two big lessons from those failed transactions. The first was resilience. I now have that in spades. Back then though, having poured months and months of work into something only to see it unravel in front of you, I often found it hard to see positives in what appeared to be failure. But I learned to take it on the chin, brush it aside – and move on. That particular experience became the foundation I later used as a springboard to achieve my sporting ambitions.

The second lesson that was hammered home to me was the necessity to give every business goal *respect*.

A large part of that respect meant never taking my ambitions or goals for granted. It meant delivering what I set out to do – not an ounce less. Getting to the finishing line was the deal. I had to do everything in my power to keep going until I had crossed it. I was aware though, that there were times when I might be tempted to try to get away with less.

It is important to realise that despite your best efforts, there will be times when things will fall through regardless of your efforts. I learned to look back positively, knowing I did everything inside of *my* control.

I have filed all this hardened education under a heading of having *respect* for my goal. As a consequence of this philosophy, I now always endeavour to follow through to the best I can on my training plans – be they business, sport or education.

I never take it for granted that I will succeed. I will not try and get away with 95 per cent because those final five per cents often contain the translation from nearly achieving to actually hitting your boiling point. Water doesn't boil at 99 degrees, but it can drive steamers and change the world when it gets that final degree of heat.

That is why I look to hit 100 per cent commitment in what I do and I encourage others to do the same. It is not something that comes naturally to us – we have to work at it.

I'm asking you now to make a pledge to yourself, that in future you avoid taking even the tiniest short cut. If you are immersed in a challenging goal, the very word *challenging* suggests it is going to test you. On a few occasions, I have seen some people not respect the goals they had signed up for. As a consequence they invariably fell short. In assessing how they did, I believe if they were really honest with themselves, they would admit that it wasn't the goal that beat them. It was their lack of respect for it.

It might be taking the goal for granted and only giving 90 per cent when it demanded more. It might be in taking on an unrealistic goal before you have climbed some lower rungs of the ladder. It might be by skipping a session or a meeting and convincing yourself it won't matter.

It almost certainly will.

Back in my 1980s school days, my exam results weren't very good. Now that I am older and wiser, I can see why I didn't do better. I thought it was because I was academically challenged, but that wasn't the reason.

I just needed to have more respect.

◆　　◆　　◆

In 2009, I went to a person for advice on the ambition I had to run 32 marathons in 32 successive days around the island of Ireland. This person had a Bible-sized book of experience in the ultra-running world.

"Do you think it can be done?" I asked him.

"Yes, I believe it can," he calmly replied. "But respect it. Respect the ambition and respect the training it will take."

Looking back now, I realise it was the best advice I got.

2

GRATITUDE ATTITUDE

**'Getting' to do something is the true
blessing that we often forget in life**

WE live a life full of habits and limitations that only change when we hear of how others have broken through those myths to achieve almost unbelievable results.

I was amazed some years ago when I first encountered people who rose above the norm to contemplate and undertake sporting challenges. The world told them that something was beyond their capabilities – but they didn't listen.

I'm thinking specifically of Terry Fox attempting to run across Canada back in 1980 after he had lost a leg to cancer. The news that would have broken so many of us inspired this young man to find an undiscovered hero inside. That took an awful lot of self-belief, but also an attitude that some people sometimes find in adversity.

Back in 1980, at the starting line in St John's Newfoundland, Fox was in no doubt of the challenge that confronted him. On top of wanting to run more than 3,000 miles, he was also trying to raise Can $1m for cancer research.

In addition to the effort required to complete such a

distance, Fox had the added problem of being a leg amputee – a consequence of developing bone cancer in his right knee. The prosthetic leg offered evidence of the additional challenge facing him.

I was immediately inspired by Terry Fox, just as much as I was by Dick Hoyt, who completed an Ironman-distance triathlon – but not in the same way others had done, before or since.

Hoyt was in his late fifties, but he wasn't alone as he entered the water to begin the Ironman triathlon. Training alongside him in the months before was his son Rick – a college graduate in his mid-twenties, who suffered from cerebral palsy since birth.

So in addition to swimming 2.4 miles, cycling 112 miles and running a full marathon of 26.2 miles, Hoyt senior carried his wheelchair-bound son every inch of the way. Older than many grandfathers at that stage, Dick dragged his son in a dingy while completing the swim. Then he cycled with Rick positioned up front in a specially-designed chair at the front of his bicycle. For the marathon, he pushed Rick in a specially-designed wheelchair. It took this pioneering father and son duo, more than 15 hours to finish their incredible challenge.

Watching the videos of the Hoyts and Terry Fox brought tears to my eyes. I was heavily involved in sport before then, but these stories educated me like no academic professor ever could. Instantly they made me realise that I could interpret my sporting activities completely differently. Before I heard of these exploits, I used to speak a language that is now redundant in my life. For instance, I would tell myself that "I *have* to run tomorrow."

Here are some other examples of a language I used to speak.

I would say that, "I *have* to swim 100 lengths in the pool tomorrow morning."

When chatting with friends about preparing for an upcoming marathon, I might say, "I *have* to run 20 miles this weekend."

Terry Fox and the Hoyts helped to change my outlook totally. They made me realise that I don't *have* to run, that I don't *have* to swim and I don't *have* to cycle. I don't *have* to take on sporting ambitions such as running consecutive marathons, or attempt ultra-distance triathlons for that matter either. I don't *have* to do any of it.

Instead, I realised I was blessed by *getting* the opportunity to do these things.

In 2009, I was sidelined from activity for almost five months because of injury. Running was temporarily impossible after a knee operation and an unequivocal warning from my surgeon that rest was best, if I didn't want to do myself long-term harm. I was despondent at the time because I missed running so much. Every day I promised myself that when my injury healed, I would remember to be grateful that I would *get* to run again. Every day I promised myself that on my return, I would always treasure the gift of simply having the health to run. So many others, including some close friends, are not as lucky as I am. I also wanted to do so as a mark of my great respect for – as well as a tribute to – the Hoyts, Terry Fox and many others like them.

I am pleased to tell you that down through the years I have kept this promise. It was a blessing to become aware of feeling privileged to *get* to run. It is an attitude that I have since brought into all aspects of my life – and it has changed my life profoundly.

Not only do I *get* to compete in sports, I now *get* to work, I *get* to run my own business, I *get* to give talks, *get* to meet deadlines, *get* to source new clients, *get* to write, *get* to speak at conferences, *get* to travel, *get* to meet friends for coffee, *get* to clean my house and I *get* to keep my garden tidy (although the latter doesn't rock my world). After I write this, I *get* to study for academic exams which I am immersed in.

Before this, my mindset told me I *had* to do it all. Now I realise I don't.

I *get* to.

Three words that liberated my views and gave me a deeper understanding of being thankful for what I had.

Here is another big one. A lot of us have an attitude that growing older is not something to be greeted with a smile.

I disagree.

Do I have to be 48 on my next birthday or the big 50 in three years' time, or do I get to? Growing older is a privilege denied to many. Thankfully I woke up to that realisation a number of years ago. A few people I have met in life will never be 48. Destiny for whatever reason deemed it so. Be grateful that you have another birthday or the next milestone coming up.

This *get to* concept is a very simple theory and is one I have to constantly practise. I am alive and healthy and as long as I am always consciously aware and grateful for such gifts; then this is an excellent starting point to any day.

Sadly Terry Fox didn't get to finish one part of his ambition. Half-way across Canada the cancer returned and took this inspirational young man from us. His efforts and legacy though, have remained a true inspiration to generations who have heard his story. Fox's legacy is that since his death, his foundation has raised more than Can$20m through the 'Terry Fox Run', a series of events held annually all over the world. Perhaps you got to run in one. If not, perhaps you will make it your business to *get* to take part in one in the future.

I am delighted to report that those remarkable Hoyts

continue to do what they do. Following their progress provides me with a constant reminder to speak this new language and to have that gratitude attitude every single day.

Do you '*have to*' do your goal or do you '*get to*'?

I realise now that for me, it is always the latter.

One simple word changed in a sentence, transformed my life.

3

A VISION TO BEHOLD

**By seeing what will happen in your mind,
you create your own future history – here and now**

I CAME up with an idea to run 32 marathons in 32 days some years ago. Within minutes of conceiving it, I closed my eyes and pictured what I envisaged the finish line would look like. I vividly saw a powerful image of the town park in Mullingar – my hometown. I could see family and friends gathered all around. In that vision I looked tired, but I also had a picture of total happiness and contentment radiating from my face.

Within two years, this dream and vision had taken significant legs. By the time the dream became a reality, another person had joined me – Ken Whitelaw. Ken and I then shared every minute of that massive ambition together. It took two years of training and logistics preparation (we made it a public event) but on August 2, 2010, we lived the vision I had conjured up, when we entered the town park in Mullingar and crossed the finish line of our 32nd consecutive marathon.

Of course it didn't just happen. From conception to final preparation for the challenge, every ounce of our motivation and commitment was tested. We hit hundreds of walls and obstacles on that journey, as we pieced together what became a huge event.

One of the many reasons we were successful was the following.

Every time we hit what appeared then to be an insurmountable problem, I simply closed my eyes and reconnected with my original vision. That picture of entering the town park became an overpowering motivator and the reason why I couldn't and wouldn't accept failure. Ken and I didn't offer ourselves a choice.

Two years in advance and many times on the journey, I visualised not just the place, but also who would be there on the last day.

I saw the registration tent, the start line gantry being erected, I heard the music and I saw marshals and volunteers who had come to help. I saw the finish line and I saw the medals being handed out to finishers. I saw my family and my friends and hundreds of others who would be there. I even saw the expressions on people's faces. That vision provoked a surge of emotion every time and it became a sustaining energy that helped ensure my vision would be brought to life.

If it worked for Ken and I, let me suggest how it can work for you.

Start by creating a vision in your head of what success looks like to you. If it's a big city marathon, picture yourself crossing the finish line in your city of choice. If opening your own business is the goal you want to hit, close your eyes and see yourself in your new office or building.

But don't allow it to become in any way vague. Go deeper and see where you are. Who is with you? What does the office look like? Who are your customers? Picture them entering your business premises and trading with your new company.

If it's an academic goal you've chosen to pursue, close your eyes and visualise the day you pass your exam or graduate. What does the graduation hall look like? What are you wearing? Who is there? What does the scroll/parchment look like? Can you read the words on it? Can you see yourself holding it now?

If you don't think this has value, consider the words of Walt Disney, when he spoke about the idea he had to create and build what we now know as Disneyland.

"Always remember," he is quoted as saying, "that this whole thing started with a picture in my head of a mouse."

I use this device in all walks of life for one simple reason – it works. When I first decided to create a speaking and business training company, I closed my eyes again and created a vision of what success would look like. When I did, I saw myself dressed in a grey suit and sporting a blue shirt and tie. I saw myself addressing the employees of a corporate client too. I was on a stage with a lapel microphone and I had a giant television screen behind me to display images related to the presentation. I pictured a large audience in front of me and I even heard my voice.

Within a year of seeing it, I was earning my living doing it. So, what's your picture?

◆　　◆　　◆

Let me offer you one final story to offer firm evidence of the value of having a vision.

A few years ago, I met up with a friend and his 17-year-old son who had lost the motivation to do well in his final school exams. A long-term sports injury had affected him to such a degree that it had impinged on his study.

For the first 30 minutes we spent together, he was distant

and slow to engage in conversation with me. He loved sport and was quite obviously missing those happy endorphins that exercise offers. He was honest enough to say that he had lost his motivation.

I asked him a very direct question: "Why are you in school?"

Immediately his demeanour changed. He sat up in the chair and became much more engaged as he shared his ambition to go to university. He even spoke about a course he was keen to study.

I asked him what his vision of success looked like. Where did he see himself a year from now? He mentioned a particular university and with a first sign of passion in his voice, he talked about the front arch above the main entrance to the college.

I suggested to him, he go home and download an image of the front of the university. It might – I suggested – reignite his motivation to do well in his exams. I also recommended that he keep this image in front of him, wherever he studied each night.

Ten months later I bumped into his proud dad who told me that the previous week his son had walked under that arch and into the university to begin a four-year degree course. His renewed and increased study efforts had earned him the points he needed to fulfil that ambition.

◆　　◆　　◆

Having a vision of where we see ourselves in our goal is a powerful motivator. Whether it is a finish line somewhere on a run course, playing sport in a stadium full of people or passing an exam in an exam hall, it can work for you. It could be as simple as seeing yourself delivering a work presentation or signing a contract with a new client next year. Or it might be seeing yourself seated in the office of your future employer and working at your dream job. It might just be you on stage singing to an audience or travelling to a far-flung destination. It's your vision and your goal and all you are doing is showing yourself a glimpse of your own future history.

Keep that vision to the forefront as you travel the journey. When you hit a wall or two – as everyone does – simply reconnect with your vision. That will drive you on to your destiny and boy will you enjoy it, as and when you get there.

4

FOR THE 'NEW' GOOD TIMES

**Dwell not on your shortcomings, but
recall instead your achievements**

I WATCHED a television documentary where the great Irish playwright and novelist, John B Keane, was interviewed about his life and times. This proud Kerryman produced some of Ireland's greatest ever plays, some of which tempted Broadway producers to come knocking on his door. One of his most famous creations, *The Field*, was turned into a Hollywood film blockbuster starring John Hurt and Richard Harris.

As the credits rolled on the television documentary, Keane was asked about his proudest achievements. His reply wasn't what you might have expected as he didn't mention a book or a play. Given more time I am sure they would have been high on his list, but he picked only one achievement. It had happened decades before. In 1950, at the age of 22, he had scored a point in a tournament final involving his local football club.

As he disappeared from the television screen more than 40

years after that football game, the pride of that achievement still poured from his chiselled face. It had meant that much to him.

The relevance of this introduction will become apparent as you read on.

◆　　◆　　◆

Is your goal a half-marathon, a college course, a job promotion, to find a new partner, save a financial sum, win a trophy, overcome a fear or trek the Camino De Compostela?

Different strokes for different folks.

One of the many things I see in my line of work is people's opinions of themselves. Often, people put themselves down simply by the words they use or the disregard they have for past achievements. We can be very quick to downplay our previous successes or even dismiss them totally. Many doubt themselves about future ones too. It shouldn't be so.

As an exercise, take out a pen and paper right now.

Are you ready?

Ok, when you are, I want you to think about the things you are most proud of in your life. What have you already achieved? Maybe it's an academic qualification; maybe you've raised children and provided for them at every turn; maybe you won a job over other candidates; scored a crucial goal or saved one at the other end; got a great job; climbed Mount Kilimanjaro; or did your local sprint triathlon.

Did you learn to speak another language, complete a computer course, grow a company, win a sales award, start a blog, take up walking, change your eating habits, redesign your garden, overcome an illness, nurse a family member or pay off your mortgage?

I want you to go into your mind to remember things that might have happened last week, last year or in the last century. It doesn't matter when. Take a few minutes to think and then list the things that come to mind. Try to list four or five at least.

See you when you're done.

◆   ◆   ◆

So what did you write down? What are you most proud of?

Now that you are finished, you can put the list away if you like, but I recommend you don't. I recommend you keep it visible – hidden from others if you wish – but visible to you. I also highly endorse never, ever erasing this list from your mind. It shows what you can do and what power you possess.

Why did I ask you to do this exercise?

Well, I am now of the belief that success is 80 per cent in the mind. Take it from someone who once thought – as an example – public speaking was impossible. Now it's my business and one of my passions. That's quite an about-turn. Once I was so petrified of it (2005), I had to go to a hypnotist to find the courage to address an audience of four people. I thought it was impossible for me. It is the biggest achievement of my life to date, as it was the hardest to do.

I believe success is hugely influenced by our state of mind and unfortunately many chose to focus largely on negatives. We talk ourselves down and refuse to take a compliment. We dismiss our value. We downplay our achievements.

Here is what we often hear.

"Ah no, don't thank me, it was nothing." *"It was only 10km."* "Yeah, but look what she did." *"It was only such and such."* "It was no big deal." *"Yes, I did three, but she got four."* "That was years ago." And finally, *"I know I scored two goals, but did you see the one I missed?"*

We think it's the humble thing to do. Or we just find it hard to have other people say good things about us. We downplay or dismiss as insignificant what might have taken enormous effort on our part.

I am all for humility. I am not suggesting you go around with a loudhailer proclaiming you can speak Spanish or did a half-marathon. But do so in your mind. You wrote these things down because they meant something to you. If you don't believe me, reflect for a few minutes on what it took to achieve them.

Was it four years of college studying for hundreds and hundreds of hours? Was it keeping your business going during the downturn? Was it overcoming an illness? Was it raising a family under a challenging situation or time? Was it embracing exercise to get you back on a road to a healthy lifestyle when the much easier thing to do was to do nothing? Was it being there for someone when it didn't suit? Was it standing out from the crowd when the easy thing to do was to stay back? Was it something that took huge bravery?

If I were doing this exercise, amongst other things I would write:

- I got a D in Pass Maths (minimum grade required to pass) in my final year school exams (1985);
- I overcame a pathological fear of public speaking;
- I've been a Business Owner for more than 12 years.

Jack Canfield, the American motivational speaker and co-author of *Chicken Soup for the Soul* was apt with his quote on self-evaluation: "By taking the time to stop and appreciate who you are and what you've achieved, you can actually enhance everything about you. Self-acknowledgement and appreciation are what give you the insights and the awareness to move forward towards higher goals and accomplishments."

So, what to do?

In the interest of using this past success to help you achieve future goals, why not recall them at strategic times – in your mind. Why not use this when you are faced with another challenge or you doubt your ability to achieve something new. Sports people constantly remind themselves of how good they are so as to achieve new goals. So why shouldn't we for goals outside of sport?

It might also be useful to give these past achievements a number in terms of difficulty. If it took a lot, give it an eight or a nine. If it took a huge amount of sacrifice and effort, give it a ten.

I did this exercise once with someone who had a big work challenge. They were very stressed and worried about something, so I encouraged them to think about the things they were most proud of. They immediately thought of something health related. I encouraged them to reflect on what it took to get them through that. Immediately they became quite emotional and gave it a resounding ten. When I asked them to give the work challenge a number by comparison – which minutes before they were troubled by – they had to honestly give it a three.

If I'm faced with a challenge now, I just close my eyes and recall that first public speaking success. In terms of difficulty, I would give it a ten. It took everything I had. Rarely now do my goals or challenges reach a five or six. Sometimes I give them a number and link back to numbers I have given those previous achievements. Then I compare them and it cements a belief that I have what it takes to achieve this new goal.

Have a great feeling and attitude about what you have already achieved in your life and never forget it.

It can help you secure future success.

FOR THE 'NEW' GOOD TIMES

5

MEASURE BY MEASURE

The real benefit of achieving your destination in stages

A FEW years ago I enjoyed reading the weekly blogs of three people, all of whom were preparing to run a marathon. The blogs were very enlightening into what each was undertaking as they travelled their individual journeys. As they progressed through their training programmes, each of them experienced more highs and lows than a theme park rollercoaster.

For many of us, the marathon or indeed any big goal we might attempt, is our equivalent of scaling Mount Everest. I believe there can be alignment in comparing our own ambitions with those climbers wishing to conquer the world's highest peak. Most mountaineers wishing to climb Everest do so from the side of the southwest ridge. To reach the top, they go through five stages.

The first sees them reach base camp at 17,700 ft. In this instance, we may liken reaching base camp to us getting up to a basic level of fitness or writing the first draft of a new book. Once they get to base camp, the mountaineer generally stays there for several weeks to regroup, acclimatise further whilst preparing for stage two. That makes sense and even when we are on our own less vaunted journeys or goals, sometimes we need also to acclimatise to the new height we have reached as well. In other words, don't try and push yourself further before you are ready.

From base camp, Everest climbers ascend to a height of 19,900 ft, where they regroup once more. If you are preparing for a marathon, perhaps this is where you reach double digits on a training run for the first time. They have reached the next phase at a measured pace. So should we. Some people often try to do too much too quickly and fall down as a result.

For the climber, the terrain gets a little trickier from here. If our own goal is really challenging, then similarly it will start to ask many questions of us too. Climbers hoping to reach the summit have to get fitter, eat better, rest and generally be positive about each day's exertion.

When you think about it, this should apply to us. We all need to be fit for our goals.

Camp Two on the world's highest peak is at 21,300 ft. What's the equivalent for you? If you are preparing for a half-marathon, this is perhaps the eight-mile point in training or 16 miles for a full. It could be writing a new business plan for a bank, completing year two of an academic ambition or sitting the first round of a job interview that you have prepared well for. We are now entering the next phase of our goal and are being asked some slightly more challenging questions. We must answer them well.

This is when the climber takes stock of where they are. They regroup by resting a little more and harness a positive mind-set to reach Camp Three (24,500 ft).

To reach it, fixed ropes are on the mountain to guide and assist. Maybe at this point, you too might need some extra help. How does that look for you?

By now the climber is just 500 feet below Camp Four and the South Col, but they are perched on a small ledge. The heights here can be daunting and I am not just speaking of the climber.

Here, the marathon runner is just a day out from running their first marathon; the student is days away from their final exams; the first-time author is now organising her book launch; the entrepreneur is days away from launching his new business.

Once here and before the final assault, the climber regroups one final time. Then the moment of reckoning arrives. That is the day we push ourselves further and higher than ever before, to scale our chosen mountains.

Many climbers have reached the top of Mount Everest.

So can you.

6

SOUNDING THE RIGHT WHISTLE

If you want to be successful in your field,
why don't you talk to those who were already there?

BEFORE me were 96 people. All were dressed casually, unlike the black clothing they normally sported. It was early 2012, many months before these guys did what they did best – referee big games.

When I asked them their ambition, they pointed outside. As I glanced to my left, I could see the green hallowed turf of one of Ireland's most hallowed sporting arenas. Croke Park is home each September to the All-Ireland football and hurling finals, whereupon 80,000 passionate fans congregate and fill the stadium. England has soccer, West Indies has cricket, America has baseball, Ireland has the Gaelic Athletic Association (GAA).

We were ensconced in the Croke Park stadium for a two-day conference. These referees were the best in the country and were now responding to my question – they were telling me why they did what they did. The ultimate goal for them, they said, was to referee in Croke Park in September. It was their Holy Grail.

I offered them a strategy to help them achieve their goal. I had shared the same approach with a group of 50 insurance brokers just a few weeks before – all of whom wanted to grow their businesses.

I was well researched in advance of meeting those knights of the whistle. My simple aid to them that night was: 'Find someone who has done it.'

Here is a short extract from my presentation.

"I am now speaking to 89 of you..."

Then I paused because I wanted to drive home my main point.

"There are seven people in this room who have already done what it is you want to do. They are sitting among you right now. Why don't you go and ask them how they did it? Why don't you ask them for advice? Why not ask them if they would mentor you? Why not ask them for the greatest lesson they have learned? If you are genuinely serious about your ambition and are keen to explore a possible strategy to get you there, I wouldn't be leaving this two-day conference without asking them for help."

I had conveyed a similar message to 45 of the 50 insurance brokers. Forty-five of those business people were having a really tough year, yet in the same room there were five others who were having their best ever year. Those five were proving what was possible. I suggested to the 45 that they go ask one or more of the five for advice or mentorship.

Of course, there was the possibility that competition or shyness might hinder an approach, so I tried to cover that off too.

"If that's the case, why not study their behaviour from afar?" I suggested. "What are they doing that you are not doing? What are they doing that you can learn from? Success leaves clues."

One of the seven referees (who had already taken charge of an All-Ireland final) had previously shared his strategy with me. He told me years before, he had identified four role models, all of whom had refereed a September final. By studying what they did, he identified what they were especially good at.

From one, he learned the value of remembering players' names. It helped build rapport and respect. Another was to become exceptionally fit – a vital component to the job when making decisions under pressure. A third was to develop and maintain a cool persona on the pitch. The fourth one he studied had developed an exceptional ability to control heated situations. Through repeated practice, he added all of these skill sets to his own armoury. A few years later he was selected himself to referee on the big day.

Of course, there was more to it than that, but bear in mind, there are only two referees chosen each year – one for football and one for hurling. The odds are stacked against them. This man knew he had to leave no stone unturned in his quest.

And therein lies a strategy. If you are looking for a way; if you are stuck; if you have hit a wall; if you can't figure out how to advance your ambition or objective – find someone who has already done it. Ask them for advice, read their book or study what they did.

Maybe you want to run a marathon in under 3:30. Maybe you want to learn how to present with confidence. Maybe you want to write a book or run an online business from the comfort of your home. Maybe, like Tony Ryan back in the 1990s, you want to run a profitable airline.

If you want irrefutable evidence of the value of this strategy, here it is...

At the time, Ryanair (an airline Ryan had co-founded) was anything but profitable. Tony Ryan was a very clever businessman though, and knew the value of learning from those who had been there and done that. So he dispatched one of his key staff members – Michael O'Leary – to Dallas, Texas, to spend time with a man called Herb Kelleher. Ryan's instruction to O'Leary was simple – "Go and learn from him."

At the time, Kelleher was CEO of Southwest Airlines. Southwest was and continues to be one of North America's most successful airlines. Given that Ryanair was operating in a market on the other side of the world, Kelleher was more than happy to meet with O'Leary.

In 2012, by then in his eighties, Kelleher gave an interview to an Irish newspaper. This was his recollection of their encounter:

"He [O'Leary] was very intense about his questioning. There was no doubt that this guy was totally focused and on a mission."

In Paul Kilduff's book *Plane Speaking*, O'Leary recalls his own version with characteristic colour:

"We went to look at Southwest Airlines in the US. It was like the road to Damascus. This was the way to make Ryanair work. I met with Herb Kelleher. I passed out about midnight and when I woke up again at about 3am, Kelleher was still there, the *******, pouring himself another bourbon. I thought I'd pick his brains and come away with the Holy Grail. The next day I couldn't remember a thing."

O'Leary was joking, of course.

He remembered everything.

O'Leary returned to Ireland soon after and began implementing the clues to success that Kelleher had shared with him – dedication to a niche market, satellite airports, turnaround speed of aircraft, and a one-class, no-frills service model.

The rest, as the expression goes, is history. Two decades on, Ryanair are carrying almost 100 million passengers a year and is now one of the most profitable airlines in the world.

Looking for a vital clue to get you to your goal?

It can be as simple as finding a role model and doing what they did.

Success leaves clues.

7

EXERCISING 'EARLY' WILL MAKE YOUR DAY

Clear your day for take-off - before breakfast

THE benefits of physical exercise are well documented. Personally, I believe that every time I undertake some form of physical exercise, I always feel better.

But don't just take my word for its value and importance. Over 2,500 years ago, the Greek philosopher Plato said: 'Lack of activity destroys the good condition of every human being. Whole movement and methodical exercise save it and preserve it.'

If you're looking for a new key to a better you, then embrace physical exercise. If you want to reach your best in all aspects and to get the most out of each day, I challenge you to go further. If you want to feel more positive throughout each day and if you want to reach your best on a consistent and daily basis, exercise in the early morning.

Having bundles of energy after an evening workout is great, but where do you bring all that energy afterwards? Why not have that feeling before you go into your normal routine? That way you will be bursting with energy and heightened enthusiasm to tick off your 'to do' list that day. Of course you might wish to train in the evenings too as part of a planned session with a group, but it doesn't mean we can't wake the body up with something that gets you moving first thing. It might be a walk or a jog, a five-minute jump on a garden trampoline or some regular strength and conditioning exercises.

I believe exercise at any time of the day is great but by doing it early, we create a launch pad in terms of physical energy that will assist you with the goals you are trying to achieve throughout each day of your life.

Even if you feel you don't have the time for early morning exercise, try and make the time. You will find time for anything you are committed to.

I truly believe it will change or improve your outlook and it will change or elevate your mood every day. You will feel more energised, more upbeat, more positive, more committed and more confident that you can achieve all of your other goals. And you'll feel better too, maybe even a lot better.

The experts will tell you that 30 minutes is optimum. That represents only two per cent of your day. Yet it's a huge key to the quality of the other 98 per cent of your daily life.

Exercise at any time of the day is good, but doing it in the early morning, in my book, is invaluable.

If you don't believe me, try it a few times next week. You will see and feel the benefits almost immediately and it will get you closer to your goals.

8

LIGHTING THE WAY

Just ask your mind to conceive, then believe to achieve

THE South African golf professional Gary Player has been a role model for millions throughout his illustrious career. At the time of writing he is fitter than many half his age – even at 79. Many people choose not to embrace the advantage that being physically fit can do for their ambitions. Oh boy, are they missing a big piece in the jigsaw. Always mentioned as being among the most successful golfers of all time, Player, despite his autumnal years, still does 500 press-ups a day.

In researching the nine-time Major winner, I came across three rather apt quotes attributed to him. They are particularly fitting if we are reading them whilst pondering an ambition or a goal. The first Player quote is self-explanatory because of the level of truth contained in it. He once said: "Simply by making the effort to start something, you will be miles ahead of almost everyone else."

This is a simple theory, but so very true. So many people want and wish for something but never take the first step on the journey. Goals and achievement do not come to us. We must go to them.

His second quote goes a long way towards answering the question of why some people seem to reach great heights. It is perhaps his most famous sound bite.

"The more I practise, the luckier I get."

So often we know of people who exceed their talent. This is perhaps their secret. Many of the necessary keys to achieve success are just hard and smart work, as well as repeated practice. There was no shortcut for Player and we need to realise this. If something is going to challenge us, then it will probably ask every question.

I firmly believe that the amount of effort we put into something will go a long way towards determining the level of satisfaction and success it provides in return.

Player's third quote was the following: "We create success or failure on the course primarily by our thoughts." He was talking about a golf course, but this kind of positive thinking applies to any 'course' in life.

We must believe we can achieve our goal. It is fundamental to success. By picturing us doing so and the steps we must take to get us there, we then act out what we already have created in our mind.

The early 20th century author Napoleon Hill – in referring to achievement – once wrote: "What the mind can conceive and believe, it can achieve."

Three quotes to success or was that four? They are all worth remembering – and all worth applying too.

9

SMALL STEPS, BIG FOOTPRINTS

**How to overcome that challenge you
think is so big, that it's impossible?**

JOHN NABER was from Illinois in the United States. In 1972 he was an 18-year-old freshman in college and holder of a national swim title. Around that time he was also inspired by watching Mark Spitz win seven gold medals in the Olympic Games in Munich. From this inspiration, Naber identified an ambition to win Olympic gold in the 100 metre backstroke event at the Montreal Games (1976).

Let's be clear about this – Naber's ambition was considered off the wall by many at the time. The winning time in 1972 was 56.58. Naber's fastest ever time over the same distance, was just under 60 seconds – a colossal shortfall.

On top of that, he predicted (rightly) that by the time the next Olympic Games came around, 56.58 seconds was unlikely to win gold. So he set himself a target of 55.5 seconds, meaning he had to swim more than four seconds faster. While it appeared on paper to be an impossible task, the strategy he adopted to get him there has since become the stuff of legend.

Let me share with you what he did.

◆　　◆　　◆

Looking at an improvement of four seconds in one sitting seemed impossible, so he resolved to break it down into gradual progresses.

Firstly, he focused on the four-second improvement with the aim of getting faster by one second per year. He knew if he did that, he would be able to swim the distance in 55.5 seconds.

He knew he wouldn't train for 12 months each year so he factored in that he would take eight weeks off each year. This meant he would spend 10 months of the year training so his calculation showed he would need to improve by one-tenth of a second for every month of his actual training.

Then he analysed his improvement journey even further. Training six days a week (not seven) he undertook to improve by an average of 1/130th of a second over 100 metres every day he trained.

He didn't stop there.

Finally, in his calculations, he quantified that he would need to train for four hours per day. As a consequence – and to make 55.5 seconds a reality – he worked out he had to improve by 1/1,200th of a second (on average) for every hour he practised.

Explaining his strategy, he said: "For me to stand on the pool deck and say 'during the next 60 minutes I'm going to improve that much (less than the blink of an eye) is believable'."

Now of course, this didn't happen every day. Life and extracting potential isn't that straightforward. I would imagine that some days it worked for him and other days not so much. But he committed to those averages of improvement and over those defined periods.

Over that four-year cycle, he dedicated himself to those incremental improvements. Four hours every day, six days every week, ten months each year and for four years.

Afterwards, Naber explained: "Four seconds of improvement before the next Olympics was too much of an improvement to visualise, but I did believe the daily goal I set myself."

Not only did he win Olympic gold, he broke the world record in the process (55.49 seconds). It took staggering commitment to the cause but therein lay two clues – supreme commitment, and a simple plan.

◆　◆　◆

So how does this apply to you?

If it's a marathon time, maybe you can get a few seconds faster in your speed sessions each week. How much more could your academic results improve by, if you resolved to improve by one per cent for every hour you studied? This could help you climb from a low D to a low C. It can work for Bs and As too.

Imagine if you brought this diligence to every hour of your working life, just how much more could you sell? How much could you grow your business by or how much improvement could you bring to your organisation?

If you're ambitious and are looking for ways to make the impossible possible, then break it down. Resolve to improve in incremental amounts. It need only be by the blink of an eye, but it can help you win your Olympic gold.

The next chapter in such a success story can be yours. It can be done.

John Naber proved it.

10

GO BEYOND, NOW

**If you are struggling at something, simply project
yourself forward in time, to how you are going
to feel when it is accomplished**

AT a corporate speaking function, a member of the audience asked me a question about an endurance triathlon that I had completed a number of years before. In that event I had swum, cycled and ran for an average of 16 hours per day – every day for 10 days.

"Surely," he enquired, "there were times when you must have doubted your ability to succeed. What did you think about during all those hours, to make sure you kept going?"

His question immediately prompted me to recall something valuable that I learned years before.

At one time in my life, I had visited a hypnotist to help me overcome a pathological fear of public speaking. "But isn't that your occupation now?" you might ask. Well, yes it is. But as recently as 2005, it was my biggest fear. My goal then was to overcome it, but at the time, it presented a huge mental barrier. I thought speaking publicly (in a stage environment) was impossible. So I sought the help of the hypnotist.

During that one-hour session he got me to focus on a time when I would be finished the speaking presentation and asked me what time that represented. I was due to speak at 3pm on the day in question, so I replied, "Four o'clock".

He explained to me that I was focusing on the fear and on what I didn't want (making a fool of myself). I was focusing on a time when I would be immersed in something that terrified me. His theory was that I should focus on a time when I would be finished. He wanted me to create a vision in my mind of what that looked like – when I had come out the other side.

As the session progressed, he got me to picture where I would be at four o'clock. When I closed my eyes, I was back on the street outside the hotel I had just presented in. In front of me was the real world; people walking the streets, cars honking, phones ringing – normal things. Now that it was 4pm in my mind, I was part of that world again and deliriously happy to be so.

His rationale was that the universe guaranteed that 4pm was coming. He also said that the universe wasn't concerned with my fear. It would continue about its business regardless. We practised some other techniques too, but this one particularly resonated. He closed the session by suggesting I stay strong until 4pm and focus solely on that.

That first official public speaking engagement (I was in a different business back then) certainly wasn't pretty. But his theory did help me hugely to get through that first experience.

Even though I doubted myself hugely, I managed to get through it simply by creating a vision of success *beyond* the finish line. I was still pathologically scared but I followed through until I reached 4pm.

Overcoming that fear was the biggest achievement of my life.

I believe this can work in any situation. If you have a huge workload ahead, picture a reward once you have it done. I went out for dinner later that night and celebrated my achievement. Think about that, but make a commitment that you only get the reward if you do the things you have on your 'to do' list.

◆　　◆　　◆

The question the man asked me at the start of this chapter, was the essence of how I tackled that 10-day sporting ambition.

There were many days when I was really struggling. There were many times when I needed something positive to focus on.

So for that reason, I focused on where I would be at 11pm.

Each morning we started at 6am, but I knew that each day, 11pm represented a time when I would be finished that particular day's test. My focus each day therefore, became 11pm.

An image of being back in the sanctuary of a sleeping bag – with another day ticked off – always came to mind.

As the 10 days progressed, later I began to focus on Sunday, June 12th. That would represent the final day. I wasn't in fear of this event but I did need something positive to focus on. I rationalised that the universe guaranteed that June 12th was definitely coming, but I had to keep moving forward, otherwise I would be disqualified. I knew that if I just kept moving forward (the one thing I was in control of), sooner or later June 12th would arrive.

If you are concentrated in the middle of a goal, there may be times when you lose motivation, focus or self-belief. If that happens, close your eyes (unless your goal involves driving a vehicle of any kind!) and attach a time to *your* finish line. Then picture yourself being there at that time. Create a vision of what that looks like.

If you're facing a big exam, picture the day after you have it finished. If it's a really heavy workload between now and June 30th, picture July 1st.

Realise that if you just keep moving forward – and critically controlling and delivering what you must – you will eventually reach your destination.

GO BEYOND, NOW

11

RECHARGING
THE BATTERY

Discovering when 'less' means 'more' in what you do,
is untapping a moment of wisdom

I RECALL a time a few years ago when I suddenly began to feel exhausted. Mid-week speed sessions, a Saturday tempo followed up by a 20-mile run on Sunday morning can do that to a body. A weekly total of more than 60 miles meant my body was like a car that was down to its final fumes of gas. I was immersed in a few other responsibilities too, most of which were just normal life goals – like a busy work diary and some family goals too.

One night during that same week I noticed the battery on my mobile phone was flashing red. A phone call that day had lasted for more than an hour, the equivalent of a 20-miler for the phone. It needed a break from the demands I had placed on it – a recharge.

When I thought about myself, I realised that my body was no different.

Sometimes when we check our phone battery late at night it might be down to 15 or 20 per cent. Seven or eight hours of recharging works wonders. I realised my body's reading was hovering near zero. It too, needed a massive recharge. The only way that would happen was if I backed off and allowed myself to recover fully. To ignore the warning signs which were so evident would have repercussions down the road.

A running friend once complained of having a few injury niggles and feeling very lethargic. I recommended he back off from his schedule for three days. He didn't listen and a week later he had to take an enforced week-long running holiday. His body was annoyed with him and this was its way of making it known. Not only had exhaustion taken over, his niggle had developed into something far more significant and counter-productive.

Very often at the peak of training (or effort of any physical or mental kind) if our bodies are saying they are tired, the sensible and most productive thing to do is to back off. That is every runner's crux – to know when to train and when to rest.

This works in everyday life too. Our body is a vehicle that takes us to our goals. If we overuse the vehicle, it will not perform at its optimum and if pushed too far, it will become very uncooperative.

So what should we do?

I learned many years ago that resting the body is a discipline in itself. That is why many marathon training schedules factor in a rest day immediately after the long run. It knows that if you have trained as planned, that is when you are most vulnerable. If you're a marathon runner, isn't it true to say that you are rejuvenated both physically and mentally after the day of rest?

This applies to every human body and any goal we might be striving for. If you are an accountant and you continue to burn the midnight oil, sooner or later your body will say enough is enough. It's the same for musicians, students, writers, footballers, taxi drivers, receptionists, fitness enthusiasts, dentists, dancers and doctors. The next morning I looked at my phone and it had a reading of 100 per cent charge. By the following weekend – as a result of two days of resting – my body felt the same.

Watch out for this warning sign while you are immersed in pursuing your sporting, business or personal goals.

Of course you need activity to reach your goals – and usually lots of it.

But resting gets you closer too.

12

GOAL SETTING

Why it's important not just to quote it - but to note it

IF you are already on your way towards achieving your dreams and ambitions for this year, read on. If you have already fallen short on last year's New Year's commitments, you should definitely read on.

Before going any further I will give you a tip that changed my life. From today on, if you begin your day by writing down your goals, it will alter how quickly and easily you can get to where you want to be.

The first time in my life I wrote down a goal was in 1999. For years before, my brother had repeated a mantra to me: "If it's not written down, it didn't happen or it probably never will." In my case, it was a golf-related goal that had been in my mind for more than 20 years. It was to reach and play consistently to a four handicap and to shoot a sub-par round in an official competition. The goal was big and I knew it would take such a huge effort. So for once, I decided to follow my brother's advice by writing down what I wanted to do.

Six months later, I achieved it.

In the heel of the hunt, that was the overriding difference

compared to all those previous efforts that had never quite happened. I was a very average six handicap before this and I had never shot a sub-par round in my life.

It's simple to write down your goals and the statistics will offer evidence that you are far more likely to achieve them if you commit them to paper. Simple, yes, but this little secret still eludes the vast majority of people who want things to change for the better but never get round to writing down their goals.

If you haven't already done so for this year's ambitions, then there is no time like... right now.

Writing down something as banal as I want to get better at fitness, health, business performance etc is ok, but for this to work you must be more specific. In my case, I had wanted to become better at that big sporting ambition of mine, but that year (1999) I got specific so that the target I wanted to reach came to life within me.

The next thing we must understand about goals is that they must have a deadline. I gave myself 12 months.

Write down very specifically what you want to achieve and then add a deadline. Here are a few examples:

I *will* (note the strong language) run a marathon by (date) in under 4.5 hours (or a 5km in under 30 minutes).

I *will* grow sales in my business by 8 per cent in the next three months.

I *will* reach grade four on the piano by 30th July of next year.

I *will* have the new house built to roof level by the last week in May.

It is also important to show yourself that you mean business to yourself, so sign your name to your goal as if it was a genuine contract.

Then it does become a contract – with yourself.

Sign it and keep it visible. Hang it on the fridge, keep it in the car, carry it in your wallet or bag. By making copies and keeping it in front of you, it will help sustain your commitment by becoming a part of your life.

You must create a plan (performance goals) around that goal too and then execute them on an on-going basis. Write and sign those performance goals too. It might sound complicated, but it's not really. In reality, it's actually quite simple – and has been proven to work.

Now you are the hunter when it comes to your goals. And your prey is success. The truth of trying to achieve your goals this way is that you are far more likely to succeed. And that success will lead on to further successes as you write them down too.

13

IT'S ALL ABOUT YOU

**Getting feedback from other people is the
best way to improve your performance**

NOT too long ago I created and began presenting my own one-day seminars, which I had spent countless months preparing content for. My goal was to create an empowering day where I would share 'daily habits' that would help those attending to realise all of their goals. It's a full-on, action-packed day that runs for nine hours and I was delighted when early feedback was very positive.

Almost three years on, that day has grown immeasurably both in terms of numbers attending and in delivery. This piece offers a clue as to why it's become more popular and more sophisticated as well.

◆　　◆　　◆

At the end of every event we hand out a sheet asking attendees for detailed feedback. We pose nine questions to get an insight into what they thought of the day. No matter how good my team and I might feel it went, the most important – and some would say the only – opinions that matter are the customers' opinions.

In this questionnaire, we try to dig deep. We ask very specific questions. We are even brave enough to ask people: "Is there anything about the event that you did not enjoy?" We are trying to get a ringside seat into their minds as to how it was for them. If there is something about the seminar that turned them off, it's unlikely that person will return or recommend the seminar unless they feel it's fixed or improved. So aren't we better off knowing about it?

Now you might rightly say that questionnaires are nothing new. You see them everywhere. Yes, that's true, but it's the standard of the questions that determines how effective a tool they can be. It also requires that we take on board any justified criticisms or observations by making the requisite changes.

Our survey is not the usual 'rate from one to ten'-type surveys. I find those one-card questionnaires that we see in coffee shops, restaurants and airports useless and often presented by people who are not really open to feedback at all. Questions are usually followed by less room for responses than is offered to a postage stamp.

We leave half a page.

I have rarely seen comments that I have made as a customer myself responded to or indeed implemented. It often strikes me that if staff see something negative or constructive, accidently they assist the questionnaires to fall into a nearby bin. Sometimes I wonder are they read at all.

Some perceive customer feedback as criticism. I view it as the probable truth. It doesn't mean I have to agree with everything, but if I feel I ought to take it on the chin, then I will.

I remember getting feedback from a corporate speaking client in my early years. He told me one delegate had complained that I spoke too fast. I reflected on the feedback and the following week I recorded myself delivering a session.

She was right, but until then, I wasn't even aware of the fact.

I was in the early stages of my speaking career back then and I saw in the video that I was nervous and the quickened pace of my delivery was due to that. That person did me a huge favour. In the weeks and months afterwards, I upped my game considerably. Now I hire someone regularly to analyse my performance. This speaking coach will tell me the truth, the whole truth and nothing but the truth. I will be told what I did right and what I did wrong and then I will ask: 'How can I get better?'

We ask that same question on the form.

How can we get better?

I rarely see this question on other feedback forms yet this question always provides us with some brilliant insights and ideas for us. That's why we ask it.

◆　　◆　　◆

The kernel of this story is to open our mind to the views of others? Why not go looking for feedback? Why not ask customers, friends, teachers, mentors or coaches about ways you can improve? Why not seek outside opinion on how you, your company or your product can become even better?

Remember, it's you who stands to benefit. Ignore it and you will either plateau or possibly see a decline in your performance over time.

It's funny how most people never see themselves as the solution to a problem. I know, because I was once that person.

It wasn't out of stubbornness; it was actually just a lack of awareness and maybe a lack of knowledge and ambition on my part as well. So often in life, I see people not willing to take advice, mentoring or guidance from other people, when it could be of enormous benefit to them.

Richard Branson, one of the most successful business tycoons in the world, says that every day he tries to learn something new from someone else.

Success leaves clues.

14

ELITE ATHLETE

**When it comes to looking after your body,
if you don't use it, you may lose it.**

ELITE athletes are the stars we watch regularly on our television screens. Elite basketball players appear at Madison Square Garden, elite baseball players hit sixes at Dodger Stadium, elite tennis players serve aces at Wimbledon, elite GAA players demonstrate their talents in Croke Park and elite marathon runners drop sweat on the streets of London, Berlin and New York.

What a joy they are to watch.

But what defines *elite*?

Well, most would say they are those of a higher class or standard in a sports discipline. Some might say professional or full-time participant.

But let me suggest and recommend a third.

I once read an article by a wise man (a retired cardiologist). In it he was giving lifestyle advice and extolling the virtues of physical exercise. When speaking about being physically active – regardless of age – he suggested that, "*If we don't use it, we will lose it.*"

His theory was that as we progress through life, the body must be continually exercised. Of course we have to modify as we get older, but he strongly recommended that we should never stop.

So for me a third example of elite is regular people who continue to exercise long after they are past their sporting prime. As I head towards 50 (still a few years away), I am determined to lead by example.

Tom Horkan, a semi-retired vet living in Mayo on Ireland's west coast, is an even better one. He is now in his mid-seventies and is the picture of good health and with a lifestyle to match. Tom continues to be very physically fit and still runs marathons. Can there be a better example of an elite athlete than he?

Another is my Dad. Even at 80+ years of age, he still swims four or five mornings a week – at least a kilometre on each occasion. He walks regularly too and he can still hit 50 golf balls with a slight fade. A stiffened back – from an accident more than 20 years ago – curtails some of his ambitions. But up to the age of 74, he was still competing on a relay team in a local triathlon.

My Dad is certain that exercising all his life has been a key to well-being and his state of good health. It has also ensured he has above average physical mobility for his age. His attitude to exercise is something I am keen to follow. It is only when he has to miss exercise for a period that he feels less able. That sentence alone is worth reflecting on and is, I'm certain, the logic behind the cardiologist's advice.

Another group I am keen to tell you about are a group of swimmers that meet at 'The 40 Foot' in Sandycove on the southside of Dublin. Every day – 365 days a year – this group meet for a daily swim in the Irish Sea. If you are unfamiliar with

Ireland's climate, be advised that this does not mean a welcoming temperature all year round.

If you ever go along, you will meet people who are in their forties and fifties. You will also meet people who were born in the 1940s and 1950s. I have even heard of one man who goes regularly who is well into his eighties.

Surely he is elite.

Whether we realise it or not, generally speaking our bodies mind us the way we mind our bodies. Whether we realise it or give it the credit for it, our bodies are always paying attention. Every day it's giving us ticks for good behaviour or an X where we have been less than good.

This is where I believe we can all become elite athletes. We should take heed of the cardiologist's wise words and continue to exercise right through life.

Our bodies want to be stretched, moved and have sweat extracted from it. At forty and fifty years of age, your body will ask: 'How did you look after me at thirty years of age and again at forty?'

At 60 it will ask those same questions. 'Did you stretch me, exercise me, move me, strengthen me and feed me with good quality food?' Yes, this principle applies to the quality of food we eat every day too. Our bodies are taking notes of that as well. The quality of our answers to these questions will in the most part, determine how enjoyable our health is a decade on.

Be aware of this now, by literally taking action every day. Similar to a person's eating habits, what you do every day is far more important than what you do once in a while. Daily exercise is important – whether it's a ten-minute walk, a yoga class, a dance routine, a swim, a stretch, a 5k run or a five-miler. What you do is personal to you. Just do whatever works.

It's always relative too. For one person, a casual walk might yield as much value as a 30-minute cycle for someone else. Remember too a statistic, from elsewhere in this book. Thirty minutes of exercise represents just 2% of your day.

Take full responsibility for this.

Your body will thank you for it, as you journey through life.

15

WHAT'S YOUR 'WHY'

**That overwhelming reason – your 'why' –
can be your secret weapon to keep going**

I AM sure that readers of this book who are into exercise will subscribe to the theory that being fit is a wonderful feeling. That energy you have coursing through your body for hours or days after a workout is an incredible gift to give our bodies. How lucky we are.

I recall once upon a time wanting a feeling like that. A poor diet however, and a nicotine addiction were too tempting a lifestyle lure though. Back in my mid-twenties, I pined for change. Almost every week, I tried to improve my diet and to quit smoking, but two days of abstinence or improvement was always defeated by a stronger opponent on day three.

I failed many, many times.

I eventually altered the direction of my life. It wasn't easy to begin the journey of losing 3.5 stone (50lbs) and giving up my daily fix, but eventually I did. In 1995, I started an exercise and improved eating regime that I've maintained to this day. The genesis for that change came from a photograph that I saw of myself, that triggered something inside to say 'enough is enough'.

We all know people who wish to change. Maybe in your case it's you, a family member or a friend. Do you know someone who wants these feelings of exercise endorphins and/or improved daily diet, but has yet to make that leap? Perhaps they have tried, but after a day, a week or a month, they have regressed.

That was me.

So what causes this and how can we get to where we want to go? I am going to share something now with you that I feel might assist. If you agree with it, please share it with others.

Whenever we identify a big goal, we should create a 'how to get there' list. These become our 'performance goals' to make it achievable. Depending on your goal, the 'how to' is the regime of exercise to help you lose weight, the taking up a hobby to keep your mind off cigarettes or the four times weekly running regime to get fit for a half-marathon. The 'how to' is vital, but often it is a feisty opponent.

If we hit a wall, I have learned there is something even more powerful we can turn to.

It is the 'Why' factor.

If you feel you are at a dead-end or find your motivation waning, sit down and think about why it is you should begin doing it in the first place. Why do you want it so much?

If your *whys* are strong enough, you will go through a wall before you will quit. My *whys* back in the 1990s were as follows:

- I wanted to stop going for a stress test every year as a result of chest pains I was getting.
- I wanted to be able to breathe like I used to at 17.
- I wanted to be able to buy clothes in the same sizes I used to fit into at 19 or 20 years of age.

- I wanted to live beyond an average life expectancy.
- I wanted to be happier than I was.

When planning something daring, alongside your 'goal' and your 'how to get there' list, write down your 'whys'.

It's not a guarantee to get you there but if your 'whys' are strong enough – and you reconnect with them when you hit a wall or two – you will go to the end of the earth before you give up.

If inclement weather conditions are keeping you from going out for a planned nightly walk, remind yourself of why you committed to it in the first place. Perhaps it's to get your health in order so you can add years to your life.

If you're having a challenging month in business, reconnect with why you are doing what it is you are doing. Maybe it's to provide a great education to your children or to retire with a secure financial future ten years earlier than most.

If you hit a wall on your academic journey, think about why you are sitting in those lecture halls day after day or night after night. I would imagine the 'why' here is to carve out a career path for decades to come, or to make yourself more attractive to your current employer or your existing clients. Rather than thinking about the 'how to' (lectures, study and exams), you can focus on that *why* instead and as a result commit to the required 'how to' list.

Know your *whys* and reconnect with them often.

They can be your secret weapon.

16

'TIME-OUT' TO SHARPEN YOUR SAW

**Do you continue to do the same thing
when it isn't yielding results?**

I LIKE a story I once heard about a man who was passing a forest one day. There he met a wood cutter who was feverishly felling trees under a hot midday sun. Sweat poured from the brow and from the upper part of the labourer's body.

"What are you doing?" asked the passer-by.

"I'm chopping all these trees down," came a frustrated reply. It was obvious he was very busy and not happy at being interrupted. "I have to be finished by nightfall."

The passer-by felt it prudent to offer some advice.

"I see the blade of your saw is blunt. Just a few miles back up the road, I passed a saw-sharpener. Why don't you go to him and get him to sharpen your saw?"

The woodcutter replied almost with a sense of outrage. "I'm much too busy. I have to keep working. Stop interrupting my work," he groaned as he returned to his task.

And therein lay the crux for many of us. Have you found yourself acting like the woodcutter, when there was a much simpler option available? Often the best use of our time is to down tools and to stand back. It might only be for 10 minutes, 10 hours or 10 days. But its impact can be enormously beneficial.

◆   ◆   ◆

One of the best lessons I ever received – if I hit a wall en route to my goals – was during the time Ken Whitelaw and I were immersed in piecing together the 32 marathons in 32 days ambition. On top of that adventure, we were also trying to raise a six-figure sum for charity.

We had publicly announced both of our goals – our strategy for fundraising was to source 1,024 people (32x32) to run with us on any one of the 32 days (we wanted to average 32 runners every day). Each of these runners would be asked to raise funds for charity, to be a part of this unique event.

Twelve weeks before the event, we were way short on our fundraising goal. It wasn't our fault – we were incredibly busy. We had work goals, family goals and there was a college course I was heavily immersed in. There was training to run 32 marathons in 32 days, finding more than 1,000 runners to join us and also a huge logistical mountain to be pieced together for each of the 32 days. Our workload was simply enormous.

We were due to start running on July 2 but in March, we had hit a wall. We were way short on the numbers of registered runners. After an initial burst of people signing up, the numbers had slowed to a trickle. Ken and I had a meeting to discuss our position. We locked ourselves in a room for two hours – just to have a 'time-out'.

Years before, I had memorised a formula for success. It highlighted four potential meeting points along the journey to reaching a goal. The first two of those were:

1. Decide what you want;
2. Take Action.

If a goal is really going to challenge us however, inevitably we will hit a third stage.

3. Notice what is or isn't working (and admit it).

The piece in brackets I have added in myself. Admitting we had hit a wall might be harder than you think. Ken and I could have made lots of excuses about how busy we were and how we were doing our best. But we knew (and we spoke about it) that if we kept our heads down and didn't change our strategy, we would still reach a finish line, but way short of what we wanted to achieve.

So often in a goal, we continue on a path that doesn't serve us best. And then we scratch our heads when we don't reach our goal. We say, "well that was the best I was capable of" or "if only we had spotted that three months ago", or "it wasn't realistic in the first place". The equivalent here for us would have been to wait until after our event to hold this meeting. Thankfully, we stood back for two hours and it had a huge impact.

What we did on reflection was, we went to visit the saw-sharpener.

Conscious or 'proactive thinking' can be a powerful strategy in such a scenario. Ken and I admitted to ourselves that we were at the third stage. We discussed our efforts and our strategies to date. We discussed what had and hadn't worked.

To re-energise ourselves, we also spoke about our *whys*. We reminded ourselves of why we were doing this, because we knew our *whys* were our motivational drivers. When we re-connected with them (there were three) it immediately heightened our resolve to get our ship back on course.

If you ever find yourself in such a situation I would encourage you to stand back, examine what you are doing and also reconnect with why this goal is so important to you. I have covered the importance and the value of having a great why, in the previous chapter.

The fourth and final stage of the formula is this:

4. Change your approach until you achieve what you want.

Up to then we hadn't made time available, but must is a great master. We knew we had to do something; otherwise we would definitely fall short of our target. Before that meeting we were on course to reach about 30-40 per cent of our financial goal for the charities.

In this conscious think-time we stepped out of the problem; we looked back in and we asked ourselves some hard questions. Is there a new way? Is there a better way? Is there a smarter way? Are we on the right road at all? Do we need to do more? Do we need to stop doing what we are doing and bring some new actions to the table? Can we? Will we? What will we do?

It only took two hours, but in that time we came up with some new ideas. One was implemented straight away and within days we saw an immediate return. This in turn ignited more enthusiasm and more ideas, which led to new interest and more registrations.

Sixteen weeks later – on August 2 – we crossed our final finish line. In the interim we had run 32 marathons in 32 successive days and more than 1,100 people had joined in running with us. As a result, the fundraising ambition we had set ourselves was not just reached, but surpassed. When I reflected afterwards, I realised that implementation of the third and fourth stages of the formula were crucial to our success.

Often it pays to visit the saw-sharpener.

Make sure to pay him a visit if you need to.

17

SMALL KEYS
OPEN BIG DOORS

Unlock your future by deciding to seize the day

A FEW years ago, I made a presentation to a group of people, all of whom were in the same profession. I was informed beforehand that they were not overly enthusiastic about their work. My brief was to talk to them for 60 minutes about self-motivation, goal-setting and strategies to help harness a positive mindset and environment.

I am sure you've heard of the Latin phrase 'carpe diem' which when translated means, 'seize the day'. I encouraged my audience to realise that if they wished to see change and to be happier at work, they could begin by choosing to change themselves. I quoted the American artist Andy Warhol: "They say time changes things, but you actually have to change things yourself."

So many people never see themselves as the solution to the problem – myself included from 17 to 27 years of age.

I got fit pretty quickly after I decided to take up running in my mid-twenties. But I got other things out of running that I wasn't even expecting. The first was I woke up to the fact that I was alive.

The old me had been sleep-walking through life in many ways, but after I bought those running shoes, I started to set a higher and more ambitious bar for myself in life. I got happier in my life too and I am certain it was because I had embraced physical exercise. As a consequence of doing exercise, I got mentally fitter which in turn encouraged me to seize every day.

The person I am now, had its beginnings back then. That is why I spent one quarter of that 60-minute presentation talking about the benefits of physical exercise and the positive impact it can have on our lives.

That same month, I addressed a workforce of a major multinational company. This firm had been actively promoting a healthy living philosophy and offered all employees the opportunity to sign up to a healthy living initiative they would provide for them. When I arrived, a quarter of the workforce was halfway through an eight-week exercise and diet improvement programme.

After I had finished, one man came up to me and offered feedback on what the programme had unlocked in him. "I hadn't exercised in 20 years but I decided to join up," he explained. "Already I have lost a stone (14lbs) simply by improving my diet and by walking four hours a week. It is the best decision I ever made."

Enthusiastically, he continued: "Before this I was stressed, unhappy and not overly enthusiastic about life. I didn't enjoy my work either. I used to see nothing but problems. But now I just see challenges to be overcome."

I was very enthused and wanted to commend him on the changes he had made, but he was keen to finish with some final words. It was actually a powerful testimonial.

"Gerry..."

"Yes," I replied.

"It has changed my life."

Those five words deserve to be reflected upon.

◆　　◆　　◆

Exercise is about so much more than the physical act. Sure, it can help you become the best 5K or marathon runner; the best cyclist, footballer, hurler or tennis player. It can also help you become the best parent, the best sibling or the best friend. Because our thoughts drive our actions – and our thoughts are elevated by exercise – it doesn't stop there.

Research shows that exercise can assist in getting better exam results, becoming happier and more productive at work, be a better sales person, engineer, guitarist, singer, chef, writer, author, orator, retail assistant, shop owner, or CEO.

For me, it is a small key that has opened hundreds of big doors.

18

FINDING YOUR
MOJO (AGAIN)

**Get your ambitions back on track by refuelling
your mind with positive thoughts**

MOJO is defined as *uncanny personal power.*

As I write this book, running continues to give me huge enrichment both mentally and physically. It is also a key to me achieving my business and personal goals.

A few years ago, I had two running goals on my radar. One was to run a personal best in a 50km event in mid-February. I had also registered for an annual 65km (39.3 miles) pilgrimage to the Connemara ultra-marathon on Ireland's western seaboard (April).

In the aftermath of the 50km, however, I totally lost my mojo for a period. My interest in training and in running waned for the first time in years. Even the thought of the Connemara ultra-marathon didn't excite my running juices.

I'm not sure what caused it but if I was to guess I would say it was a mixture of having to recover from a 50km race while remaining sharp. I was also – in the same arena of running – pursuing not one big goal, but two. This meant perhaps that my body was confused. I did manage to keep running in those weeks, but it became a chore.

Have you ever had that happen? Do you love music, but at one time or another, lost the desire to play? Do you love your career but on occasion lost a desire to go into work? Have you ever lost interest in something that you know in your heart you still love?

That is what happened to me for a brief time. Having temporarily lost my mojo, here's how I got it back.

I told myself that whether I liked it or not my training clock for Connemara was already ticking again. I reminded myself that a little over a month from then, at every mile of the Connemara Ultra, I would be asked many questions. I wanted to run a personal best there as well and I knew that wouldn't happen unless I picked myself up again.

I decided to focus on the future so as to reignite my enthusiasm for the present.

I began by reflecting on what the event meant to me. To light a strong feeling inside me, I closed my eyes and pictured myself there. In my mind, a vision of the stunning Lough Inagh Valley magically appeared. Lough Inagh was the central part of the course, a contoured valley enveloped by the Twelve Pins mountain range. Its beauty is an equal to many of the world's most famous visitor sites.

I visualised myself there a month hence, and at the start in Maam Cross. I pictured 13 miles in. I saw myself passing through the beautiful village of Leenane (setting for the movie of John B Keane's play, *The Field*) at 26 miles.

I wanted to go there and enjoy the day. I realised that the quality of that enjoyment had to be earned. So I recalled a quotation from former world heavyweight boxing champion, Muhammed Ali. Once commenting on his key to success, he volunteered, "I won all my medals long before I danced under those lights."

What he meant was, success is earned long before we do the event itself – the final day is just preparation meeting opportunity.

I knew the importance of training on terrain similar to Connemara because the Connemara course had two tasty hills to be climbed (at 26 miles and 36.5 miles). I knew that what I did in March would determine my happiness index in April, so I decided to head for a favoured hilly running environment to prepare.

Was it easy? Well honestly, no it wasn't. Did it come back instantly? Well, no again. In fact it took three or four sessions. But by repeatedly visualising what I wanted to experience five weeks later, it encouraged me into doing the physical preparation that I knew was so important. Over a short period, it definitely reignited the desire inside again. A month later I had a very happy day in Connemara. I even managed to squeeze out a personal best time by a few minutes.

◆　　◆　　◆

I believe this strategy can work for any goal. If you are struggling to focus on your studies, perhaps visualise the exam hall you will sit your exams in. If it's a heavy workload on your desk, picture a satisfied client or that big sale. If you're experiencing a loss of mojo whilst writing your book, picture it on the shelf of your favourite bookstore. If you are temporarily defeated by a lack of employment, close your eyes and picture your dream job.

Then get busy doing *your* hill sessions. Visualisation followed by actions can reignite your enthusiasm.

That's where I rediscovered my mojo.

19

PASSING THROUGH

**Know that with every challenge,
there is a mental trick to help you move on**

MY second book *Tick, Tock, Ten* (2013) tells the story of a sporting ambition I had completed a few years before. Over 10 days competitors were required to swim 24 miles, cycle 1,160 miles and run 262 miles. (It was called a DECA-Iron Distance Triathlon.) Swimming, cycling and running for an average of 16 hours a day – and for 10 days in a row – is certainly going to test every ounce of you, physically and mentally.

But isn't it the same with any really big goal or ambition?

I once met a man living in the United States. He was the general manager of a large corporate facility that often worked on significant projects that tested even the most focused of his employees to the limit. I was very flattered when he told me that something he had read in that book was now a management strategy which helped ensure they reached the end of each project.

Set out below is what he was referring to.

◆   ◆   ◆

At lunchtime on day three of that ten-day DECA-Iron event, I hit a low. My brain was having a really hard time dealing with the magnitude of what I was doing. It reminded me that we had already been swimming and cycling for almost six hours that day – yet I was still not even at the half-way stage. It then highlighted the fact that even if I finished day three, 70 per cent of this goal still lay in front of me. It was only the first Sunday and I would still be here in a week's time.

Because the body takes direction from the mind, I knew I had to source a solution – and pretty quickly at that. There and then I realised my mental resolve was being tested. I was being asked if I had what it takes and I knew I had to find an answer. The words of World War 2 American Army General George Patton came to mind: *"If you're going to win any battle, you must make the mind run the body."*

That day I conceived a mental trigger which I immediately put into action. Such was its value, I have used it since in business and in everyday life as well.

It simply involved attaching a number to my goal. Choosing a number was easy. I chose ten to represent the ten days we were required to complete.

So how might this apply to you?

Well if you're running a marathon it might be 26. In your place of employment or your business, it might be 12 to reflect the business months of the year or $100,000 (or euros) to represent a turnover target. In college it might be four to represent the years necessary to achieve a degree.

The big realisation for me was that I couldn't get to 10 without passing through three. I repeated over and over the following mantra: 'You cannot get to ten without passing through three. All you're doing is passing through.'

I told myself I had to pass through this number, that I

couldn't skip it. I told myself that this was merely one of those unexpected tests which were always going to arrive at my door – and I was now answering it. I reassured myself that in any big ambition or goal, obstacles or barriers were always likely to appear.

For you, it might be Grade Three on the piano to get to Grade Six; it might be mile 19 of a marathon to get to 26.2 miles; or it could be a tough November assignment on your college course to get to your overall qualification.

It might be completing year three exams on your way to your final year of college. It might be passing through nine handicap on your way to six in golf or it might be doing the less attractive parts of your job or business (which are important and must be done) so that you can do the parts you love and reach the figures you've targeted. For someone else, it might be some more challenging aspects of a medical recovery programme, as they restore themselves back to good health.

It doesn't have to be a number. It can be a task or even a timeline. That specific number, task or deadline might be the toughest you encounter though. I have learned the importance of being fully aware when such moments hit me and to embrace the philosophy that this is an opportunity to find out what I am really made of.

"The body is never tired, if the mind isn't tired," was the remainder of Patton's quote.

In that DECA-Iron event, this was my test and I had answered it and hardened by resolve (my mind-set) at the same time. I looked at the number of competitors that had already withdrawn and perhaps cruelly got some solace and confidence from that. I told myself: "You're still here. You're tough. Keep going."

I also knew I had to keep moving forward. That was the most

important job at hand. Three might be the toughest number, but I had to move through it. Otherwise I wouldn't get to four. I also told myself that Day Four was irrelevant. I should only focus on what I was in control of – Day Three. Why concern yourself with June exams when Christmas ones have yet to be sat.

My American-based friend explained that when it happens in their corporation now, they just heighten a resolve and a commitment to tap into a positive mind-set and push on. They remind themselves that they are just 'passing through'.

I sent my arms and legs a message to just keep moving forward. I knew that if I did so – barring injury or withdrawal – I would be guaranteed to reach 10. Eventually I passed through three, four, five, six, seven, eight, nine and ten.

Some days were harder than others, but isn't that nearly always the case.

I got there – and so can you.

Just remind yourself – you're passing through.

PASSING THROUGH

20

THOUGHT FOR FOOD

We are what we eat – and that can include the odd treat

SEVERAL months ago I bumped into a business acquaintance and friend who is one of the most motivated people I know. He is an infinite source of wisdom on many topics and we meet regularly to share ideas. This man scores exceptionally high in business acumen, fitness, motivation and goal setting. He is also a senior manager in a large company, which for him, results in having to travel quite a bit.

One of the many things I admire about him is his desire and commitment to get the best out of himself. Over the course of our chat, he confessed that he was falling down in one area – eating well. He really felt he was ticking all the other boxes, but a weekly business trip to Europe meant he was away from home quite frequently. "The reality of my work schedule doesn't allow me to eat as well as I would like. When I'm away, I don't have access to a good breakfast like I do when I'm at home. It's not good," he confessed.

He was operating at a senior business level and no doubt had significant corporate goals to achieve. I believe this is why he asked for advice. He knew that eating well was a key to having more energy throughout his business day. Eat well, perform well.

I offered him a simple strategy to solve this riddle. He appeared shocked at its simplicity but immediately responded: "I can't believe I didn't think of that."

My question to him was: "Is it possible for you to bring your own breakfast with you on the trip?"

"Of course it is," he replied. "It's just about being prepared, isn't it? I've been making excuses, haven't I?"

Before beginning each day, a healthy breakfast is a wonderful foundation to give the human body, so if you're away, don't leave it to chance. It is actually very easy to pack that basic but very important meal into a sandwich bag or box. Sure, you might get a few strange looks in the hotel restaurant at breakfast time, but who cares. Your body will thank you for it.

Whenever I am away, my own (regular) breakfast is packed neatly in beside the socks. I feel it's a vital key. If I eat well, it helps me perform well.

"But what about when I'm eating on the move in airports and such," he continued, "Isn't that more difficult?"

The truth is there is almost always a healthy option available to us if we are prepared to search for it, and make disciplined decisions. Of course it can be easy to eat poorly when on the move but if you are being honest, you'll agree that most convenience stores or eateries have shelves packed full of delicious pre-packed fruit, fish options on a variety of healthy breads and more water than is found in the River Danube.

Like most, when it comes to eating healthily, I'm no angel. But I try to eat well 80 per cent of the time, which allows for frequent treats.

Imagine eating seven apples on a Sunday to reach a weekly

intake. Doesn't really make sense does it? Just like with exercise, what we eat every day is far more important than what we eat once in a while.

Perhaps it is just about five minutes of preparation when you pack your bags, or making better decisions in the shops we buy our food in.

Everything is determined in our moments of decision.

21

NUMBERS GAME

**Don't limit your possibilities by saying you
are too old to take on a challenge**

I RECALL once being in Cork, Ireland's southernmost city. I was there on a sporting ambition.

On the way home I called into a convenience store to feed a hunger pang and whilst there I got chatting to a stranger. By the end of our brief interaction, I knew more about him than I did about Cork itself. He was full of warmth and hospitality and was obviously keen to share a pleasant word with a visitor to the area.

In that five-minute period we had chatted about the weather, we predicted the winning lottery numbers (wrongly) and, amongst other things, we talked about sport. Dressed in my running gear, I told him I was down to take part in a local event.

"Do you do much running yourself?" I asked by way of keeping the conversation going.

His brief reply gave away a lot of information.

"Yerra, I did once upon a time, but sure I'm the wrong side of 50 now for it."

◆　　◆　　◆

After we parted, his words occupied me on the way home. As I journeyed northwards I recalled someone else of his age – on the same topic – responding totally differently by declaring that "age is just a number". From people of similar vintage, how could there be such a diverse perspective?

I suppose a lot of people still think that sport is only for the younger set. But why should turning 50 necessarily be a mental milestone where activity ceases. Is it just a mindset that has been handed down to us that running isn't something you should be doing from middle age upwards?

The truth is I don't know but I am certain that for the general health of the people, this is a bad attitude to have – particularly if such a person is suffering no ill-health issues. That Cork man seemed well and didn't visibly demonstrate any ailments or physical difficulties. Yet he clearly was of a mindset that he was now past it; that running was for people younger than him.

I want to broaden this topic by telling you that running is just a metaphor in this story. I see this man's attitude almost every day in people I meet who talk themselves into not being able to do things. Unfortunately many are influenced by others' opinions. Peer pressure rules OK, but not in a good way.

Of course, to stop running is entirely his right. So is the belief that it might not be possible for him to do any more. Fortunately, others who are older are out there expanding boundaries for themselves by proving that age is no barrier to the challenges they have set themselves. As Henry Ford the American motor car pioneer once said: "Whether you believe you can or you can't, you're right."

I have referred elsewhere in this book to the importance of

role models. Go to any local run or cycle event and you will see people in their fifties, sixties, seventies and older, running, cycling or pursuing other fitness ambitions. My local cycling club boasts one of its fittest members to be 78 years old.

As I write this, I am 47, yet I feel 10 times fitter than I did at 27. I feel very fortunate to have made this happen in my life. I am also realistic enough to know that I cannot do things I could have done years ago and that's fine.

But that doesn't mean I have to stop doing things. That doesn't mean I can't learn new things or new ways to do old things.

The world is full of amazing people doing things which people half their age say can't be done. I prefer to live in their world.

It's exciting, it's challenging and it's very rewarding too.

◆　　◆　　◆

To finish, let me tell you about Fauja Singh, an Indian man resident in the UK. In 2011, he became the oldest ever finisher of a marathon.

For him, age *was* just a number.

He was 100 years old.

22

HOW TO RUN 100 MILES

**Don't practice to get something right;
practice until you can't get it wrong**

IN 2014, I decided I wanted to run 100 miles non-stop (160km). I know it probably sounds outlandish but it became an all-consuming passion for me to achieve.

Whether it is in business, education or other environments, we all get an unusual idea from time to time, which others may think either barmy or impossible to fulfil. In that journey, I secured two great learning experiences. Firstly, in plotting a route to make it possible. And secondly in what I learnt along the way.

◆　　◆　　◆

At the start of the year I knew I was fit enough to run a fair distance. Although it was a few years since I had done anything extreme on the sporting front, that January I felt I had the ability to run a marathon. The 100-mile voyage I had planned was being undertaken in August. This allowed for seven months of preparation for almost four times the marathon distance.

My plan and strategy was as follows. I plotted to run a 39.3-mile race in April, a 50-mile race in May and a whopping 62.5-mile (100km) run in June – seven weeks before my main ambition. I knew that each one of those runs would provide enormous challenges for me. The incremental increase in distance, I believed, would result in the best possible preparation.

It sounds straightforward on paper – and because it worked, I believe it has great alignment with anything that stretches us hugely on our achievement radar. It also makes not just the distance, but the preparation for the goal measureable.

Is there a value here for you? Can you identify your own benchmarks that you could hit along the way? Are there three or four milestones you could navigate to get to your 100 miles?

As an example, if it's creating a full-time speaking business that you wish to journey to, maybe it's addressing your local toastmasters group and then a local business network. If it's a football team, maybe it's focusing on winning the league en route to winning the championship. Maybe it's targeting a 12 handicap in golf to get you to single figures, or it might be years one, two and three of a four-year degree.

If you plot such a route, pretty soon you can be up past 100km on your journey to your 100 miles.

◆　　◆　　◆

April went really well as I ran a personal best in the 39.3-mile event.

So far, so good.

In June the 62.5-mile ultra-marathon (100km) also ticked the boxes.

'What about the 50-miler in between?' I hear you ask.

Well, that was a disaster.

Yes, I finished it but I made a litany of errors. On reflection though, this was the day when I learnt the most; a day when I found out what not to do if you wish to run 100 miles.

I realised afterwards, that my reaction to that day, was vital to the long-term success of my ambition. Having the ability to admit shortcomings is one of the most valuable personal development skills we can cultivate.

In business you might not be as cheerful about learning the hard way. Such errors might undermine you in a customer's eyes or cost you a relationship or a sum of money. Surely then, it is all the more reason to re-assess – as I did after that run.

That evening, I went into my own confession box for 30 minutes and while the whole experience was still fresh in my mind, I analysed and admitted honestly my shortcomings. Then I wrote them all down to keep as a reminder.

Here is what I realised:

- I had started at too ambitious a pace and only realised it at the 30-mile point. As a result I suffered a lot between miles 30-44.
- I didn't eat the right foods, I didn't eat often enough and I stopped eating way too early – 35 miles.
- I tied my shoe laces too tight. This caused significant discomfort for 10 miles.
- At 35 miles, my feet were extremely sore but I had only brought one pair of shoes. A replacement pair of shoes might have helped lift my mental state.
- I neglected to bring sun cream and it was a very hot day.
- I didn't respect the event. The items I forgot to bring offer firm evidence of this. It showed me that my focus was less than it should have been in the lead-in.

Analysing things in this manner is of huge value, yet many people continue to do what they have always done. Many are so busy denying their mistakes, they never allow themselves to learn or profit from them. My belief is that we rarely see ourselves as the solution to our own problems.

I have learned that having the courage to grow from my mistakes is an invaluable skillset to acquire. Admit my shortcomings and then do something about them. This 50-mile disaster day was my most valuable training day and after licking my wounds, I realised it.

Imagine a soccer team prior to a big final, losing a challenge match but then ignoring the mistakes they had made and repeating them in the final.

In that 50-mile run, I had prepared so poorly that with six miles to go, I wanted to stop. And I did.

I lay on the ground for about 10 minutes convincing myself that because it was only a training day, finishing was not important. I was extremely sore and I had convinced myself I risked injury.

I was soon talked into continuing by a fellow competitor who was passing by. Her encouragement gave me a lift and it was only when I got running again, I realised the brief stoppage had actually helped. From mile 44 to 50, I felt much stronger than I had an hour before, which was very significant. I realised that just because I was sore at that moment, didn't mean I would be sore for the remaining miles. That learning might serve me well if I hit a tough time at mile 70 or 80 of my 100-miler.

Initially after the race, I was a little down, until I realised the day was actually a blessing. I had served a powerful apprenticeship.

That little episode reminded me of a quote I once read: 'Don't practice until you get it right. Practice until you can't get it wrong.'

On the eve of the 100-mile run, I opened up that learnings file and reminded myself of each experience and what they had taught me. Before your next milestone, remind yourself of what you have learned. As you go along, keep a record of it.

The 100-mile run, whilst immensely challenging, was also one of the most rewarding days of my life. All of the education I secured in the lead-in meant it went pretty much according to plan.

It's what you do about obstacles that you hit, en route to your 100 miles. What determines your ability to finish is how you react to such obstacles when you do hit them, as well as the enthusiasm you bring to your subsequent actions.

Good luck with running your 100 miles or its equivalent.

It can be done.

23

HAPPINESS INDEX

**Sending positive messages to your brain
makes your day more enjoyable**

I ONCE got something stuck in my right eyelid for several hours. It was a very unpleasant experience at the time.

When I was out running the next morning I stopped for a moment to carry out an almost daily ritual. By then, full vision had been restored to my eye. Just before I finished my workout, I stopped and expressed gratitude quietly in my head for the fact that my eye was fine again. The previous day's unpleasant experience had reminded me of something which is so easy to take for granted – good health. For me, being consciously grateful for things and especially the health of myself, family and friends, is not just very important, it is also very empowering.

◆   ◆   ◆

TED Talks are an online video platform where people *share ideas worth spreading* (or so the tagline goes). In one I viewed recently, Shawn Achor, an American positive psychology researcher, was sharing what studies had claimed were the keys to happiness. This was not some random intangible and unsubstantiated opinion. This learning was based on a detailed study around attaining happiness in the workplace. It found that the keys to happiness were not bigger sales success or job promotions. When you achieve these, your brain usually just moves the goal posts to a higher level.

Rather, he suggested, the key to happiness is focusing on positivity in the present. If you raise awareness of the positivity in the moment, then your brain will seek out and find you a happier place. Put simply, it says that if your brain is positive, it will perform better than if stressed. According to his study, if we can find a way to focus on positives, we will secure higher levels of happiness and perform better in work or at home.

So how do we achieve this?

Years before (through many simple life experiences) I had been fortunate to realise the importance of being grateful for what I have every day. A knee operation and five months of abstaining from running was one such experience that led me down this road. By being consciously grateful for such blessings every day, my life has since become so much happier.

Achor's study is based on expressing gratitude for a 21-day period and beyond. In it, he suggests we express gratitude every day for three different things. You must choose these for yourself. Oh, and choose three *different* things every day.

Next he recommends that you write down in a journal one positive experience you have had in the previous 24 hours. That day was easy for me because it was when my eye felt fine again. Writing it down, though, helps us relive it.

The next element is exercise. This teaches the brain that behaviour matters. It is finished off by meditation (allows the brain to focus on a task) and a random act of kindness. For this final aspect, he recommends a simple email to someone in your social network in praise of something they have done.

That, he suggests, is a key to happiness.

The only testimonial I can give you is that I agree. By being grateful for my restored health, the following day's challenges were nothing of the sort.

I was just happy to be able to do them.

24

YOUNG SHOULDERS, OLD WISDOM

How my nephew taught me a lesson

I HAVE mentioned elsewhere in this book that overcoming a fear of public speaking was the single biggest achievement of my life. I was speaking full-time for two years before the sheer terror of it eventually faded. I don't use the word 'terror' lightly here either. I was pathologically fearful of it at one time in my life.

Even two years into it being my profession, one part of my brain was still refusing to believe I was able to do it well. Prior to walking on stage, I would be eaten up inside with fear. In some ways it was like the mental challenge I faced when trying to give up cigarettes years before. I found it incredibly hard to stay off cigarettes for the first year. I think it was because a section of my brain suddenly realised I was deadly serious about quitting and so became hell-bent on making it extra tough on me. In some ways it was saying, 'S***, he's really serious about doing this. Let's go down with a fight.'

Similarly, even though I had spoken to audiences on hundreds of occasions by then, that part of my brain was still sabotaging my mind. It had simply shifted its focus from smoking to public speaking. The jigsaw finally came together one winter. In the space of two months, I finally managed to eliminate that fear. The final two strategies were a simple breathing technique that I heard on a radio show and also the following true story which clinched it.

◆　　◆　　◆

One day I met up with my nephew Andrew, who was 10 at the time.

"Did you hear the news," he exclaimed excitedly, the words proudly revealing a smile.

"No, what?" his favourite (!) uncle replied.

"I've got the lead in the school play, *Peter Pan*."

"Wow," I responded. "That's brilliant. Well done."

Then I asked him a question of which I am not proud. I realise now it was incredibly poor judgement but I asked him:

"Will you be nervous, do you think?"

I shouldn't have asked it. It only serves to provide an insight into my own shortcomings that I assumed he might be or should be.

"Nervous, why would I be nervous?"

Ashamedly, I persisted.

"Well, there will be hundreds of people there. You'll have to sing loads of songs, won't you?"

He stared at me with a look of incredulity on his face.

"But I know I can do it," he responded simply.

I was intrigued.

"How come?" I questioned.

In the weeks after, I reflected on his response. Andrew's young philosophy gifted me a simple but powerful wisdom.

"I've already done it. I sang in front of the class last week. What's the difference?"

◆   ◆   ◆

His wisdom hit me hard. How could it not? He was 10. In that single sentence he helped draw back the curtains of my disbelieving mind.

His rationale was that audiences were one and the same. They were people in front of him who were there to listen. He had sung and they had heard. Therefore he had done it already and so he knew he could do it.

After that encounter, I went back to work on that disbelieving part of my brain. I opened up files from talks on my computer that I had already delivered. I looked at client testimonials and what they had said about my work and I resolved to pay no more heed to that side of my brain.

Within three weeks, Andrew's wisdom had helped me crush the sabotaging part of my brain. That changed mind-set, coupled with a powerful breathing technique – done for two minutes before I go in front of my audience – has worked wonders ever since.

Can you see any alignment here? Have you already done it before? In any way shape or form? Is there a way that you too can align with his philosophy?

Have you passed exams? Have you lost weight before? Have you gained a job promotion? Have you overcome a health issue? Have you won a game? Have you made a score? Have you written an article? Have you run a business? Have you reached sales targets? Have you spoken publicly before? Have you sung publicly too? Picture the evidence before you now.

It proves what power is already in you to achieve.

25

WHAT STRETCHING DOES

**Push yourself to new levels and enjoy
the process of going further and further**

ONE thing my coffee companion said, got me thinking. I wondered to myself how he would view such a distance a few months down the road.

Our conversation was held over a coffee in a quaint village shop in middle Ireland, a hamlet where the vet James Herriot might have been a resident. Seated across from me was a running convert who, as he spoke, was as excited as a 10-year-old at a One Direction concert. As the 35-year-old bit into his pastry, he began to share his experience of training for his first marathon. He had recently signed up for one and was a few months into a six-month training schedule.

"My long run this Sunday will be 10 miles. I can't believe I can run that far," he said, full of enthusiasm.

Up to a short time before, this man's daily activity involved balancing on a barstool with a cigarette constantly in his mouth. In some ways, he reminded me of the person I once was myself.

His conversion had come about some 12 months earlier, after

he had been given one of life's wake-up calls. Nothing serious, but it was enough to encourage him in a different direction.

Running seemed to offer the cure so he swapped the barstool and the Marlboro packets for canal banks and running t-shirts. Within a few weeks, running and my friend had taken to each other like the proverbial ducks to water. Talking about his long run gave clues as to who he was now becoming. Already he was a different person from just a year before.

He looks at life differently now, he told me. Previously he had no vitality and little excitement in his life. Now he was bursting with energy and was actively pursuing what were once vague ambitions in his head. His passion for this new life was infectious.

I believe my coffee companion will in the coming years find out just what amazing ability lies within him. Were we to meet each fortnight, I believe this is how the conversation might go.

"My long run last weekend was 18 miles; I can't believe I can run that far."

"My long run last weekend was 20 miles; I can't believe I can run that far."

"My long run last weekend was 22 miles; I can't believe I can run that far."

I am sure now that you know the real meaning of this story. I would love to remind him in the future of a time when he saw 10 miles as his limit. Preparing for my own debut marathon taught me so much about what I was actually capable of. Once upon a time I too experienced all of the above.

◆　　◆　　◆

All of us have dreams and ambitions but many of us doubt our ability to achieve them. If you see yourself in these words, maybe all you need is a tiny change of direction to encourage you to 'carpe diem' and to seize life itself.

We all have an ability to go beyond 20 miles, make no mistake. And the distance here is just a symbol for what we can achieve right through life, once we expand our boundaries and horizons.

For many readers, this dream or ambition might be a 5km or a marathon. For others it might be a 100km cycle. For you or your brother, your wife or your friend, it might be an academic qualification, building a house, securing a dream job, writing a book or retiring with no financial worries.

Realise that this principle can be a method in which we can achieve anything. Grow your business from €100K to €200K, the above shows you how. Go from a D grade to a C grade, it's the exact same route.

Whatever your goal, if it looks very high, just stretch yourself to go a bit further every week. But it won't happen unless you stretch.

If you do, you might be surprised at how far you can go.

26

YOUR VEHICLE

**You've gotta look after your body –
it's the only place you have to live**

ONE of my favourite motivational speakers is the American Jim Rohn. He had a brilliant philosophy on life and on what it had to offer. One of his most famous quotes: "Take care of your body. It's the only place you have to live" came to mind as I contemplated writing this chapter.

◆   ◆   ◆

One year I had a February goal to run in a 50km event. But I didn't do it.

Two weeks out from the date, training was going well. I had ticked almost every box. Just 13 days before the event however, I developed a virus that lingered for a while. As a consequence, I went nine full days without running, something which is very rare in my life.

Two days before the 50km, I was talking on my mobile phone while climbing two flights of stairs in my office building. As I reached the top, the person on the other end of the line enquired as to the state of my health. "Why are you asking?" I responded. Apparently I was breathing heavier than an overworked mountaineer.

I knew then that I had to listen to my body. Fifty kilometres (31 miles) is a hell of a distance to run. During two previous stagings, this event had tested me to the limit and I was in the whole of my health on both of those occasions.

Like me, I am sure you exercise for the challenge, for fun and for its health benefits. I realised then that competing on this occasion would be foolish.

I accepted that – despite a hunger to participate – I had to listen and respect my body. I have many other goals and ambitions in my life and I need a cooperative body to achieve them. I had to respect the signals it was sending out. So I got in touch with the organiser and gave my apologies for withdrawing.

I have learned the importance of taking care and listening to my body – just like Mr Rohn had suggested. After all, it is the only place I have to live.

If your car showed symptoms of an underlying problem, you wouldn't drive it until it was fixed. Our bodies are also a transport vehicle and we need it to take us to more than just our sporting goals.

I must take care of it and not push it when it is feeling unwell. Fortunately – when in the whole of my health – I push it to my own personal extremes. That too has a very wise strategy attached. Almost anybody can complete a marathon, but only if they put the proper training in place.

To end this message, here are some lyrics of a song sung by American country singer Kenny Rogers. Ok, so maybe he was talking about playing cards, but he might have been talking about running or – as in this case – not running.

"You've gotta know when to hold them, know when to fold them, know when to walk away and know when to run."
Listen and take care of your body.
It is the only place you have to live.

27

THE VALUE OF PHONING A FRIEND

**Get someone you trust to share your difficulty –
and watch it halve in seconds**

EARLY in 2014, I was right in the middle of a challenging period in my life. I was studying for some exams (part-time) and I also had an assignment to hand in. In my day job, I was dealing with a very busy business cycle and I had several goals outside of those as well.

My biggest problem was my assignment – I hadn't a clue how to do it. I had 50 per cent of it done, but I knew that what I had written was to a poor standard. It would have been obvious to the examiner that I had struggled with the subject and as a consequence, I was likely to get a poor grade. The deadline was looming too. Tick-tock. Tick-tock.

By coincidence I was working in a university myself that week. I had been asked to address the veterinary students of the college and arrived two hours early for my slot.

With a little time on my hands, I waited outside the lecture hall and allowed my mind to wander.

Much as I wanted to focus on my 5pm presentation, from

3pm to 4pm, all I could think about was my own college dilemma.

While I sat on the bench outside, I asked myself a question.

"If they were faced with such a dilemma what advice would you give these students you are about to speak to?"

Then a solution came to me.

Within 15 minutes I had the information I needed to get a higher grade in my assignment.

◆   ◆   ◆

So what happened in the interim?

Well, many readers will know the television quiz programme *Who Wants to Be a Millionaire*, the show where contestants get three life-lines as they try and answer 15 consecutive questions in order to secure the £1million first prize.

One of the life-lines is the option of phoning a friend and asking them for help. That is the strategy I adopted that afternoon to help me secure the prize I was trying to achieve – a high grade in my college assignment.

I rang Declan.

'Who is Declan?' I hear you ask. Well, Declan was a fellow student on my college course. The classroom consisted of busy working professionals and Declan was someone whom I had befriended. I had his mobile number in my phone, so I rang him.

Thankfully he answered the call. I explained my difficulty and what I was struggling with.

"I hear you," he said reassuringly. "Let me try and help. Don't worry. I think I understand it fully."

Even as he spoke those words I could feel my concern easing. Instinctively, I began taking notes so that I could recall his advice. The call lasted less than 10 minutes but by the time I put the phone down, my frame of mind was unrecognisable from that of the person who had made the call. In terms of value, the phone call was priceless. And I ended up with a grade I was quite proud of.

We all use the expression 'phone a friend' and we all know the value it can bring. But why is it so hard for us to do it? I had spent a week concerning myself with this dilemma. In fact, the closer it got, the more concerned I had become. By calling Declan, I had it solved in a matter of minutes.

Are you stuck on some aspect of your goal or have you hit a wall? If so, who can you call? In five years of secondary school, I never had the wisdom to ask for help. Now I am only too happy to do so. If you hit a wall on your journey, why not literally phone a friend.

People will go out of their way to answer.

You'll see.

28

INSPIRATION TO
ADD PERSPIRATION

Use those you admire in business to join yours –
in your mind game to success

THE word Inspiration, according to the dictionary, means 'animating action or influence'. When we are inspired, we are influenced to take action.

I am now of the belief that success is 80 per cent in my head and I would like to share a short piece on one of the strategies I employ.

Firstly, I picture in my mind a number of people who inspire me. They won't have any contact with me – a coach, a teacher or a mentor might be needed to help me achieve my goals, but I find one of the most powerful ways to lift myself is to think of those who inspire me.

One of the people I have surrounded myself with in the past is the inspiration of Canadian runner, Terry Fox. I have spoken about him elsewhere in this book. His story has served as a huge motivation to me with some of my past goals.

Two of my business inspirations are Michael O'Leary, the very talented, yet slightly maverick CEO of airline Ryanair, and

Brian Buffini, one of America's leading speakers on business performance, who happens also to be first generation Irish.

Often, when immersed in my own business ambitions, I picture these people in my mind and imagine them at their desks. I see them driving their respective businesses or standing on stage delivering powerful presentations to thousands of people. I then say to myself: 'Well, if they can do it, so can I.'

I am positive I have reached some finish lines in the past because of this strategy and now I encourage you to create your own list. Nowadays I think of wonderful role models like Rick and Dick Hoyt and of a man called Nick Vujicic, an Australian motivational speaker who was born with no arms and no legs. I think of my parents and my brother. I have so many role models and so many inspirational people in my mind.

At last count, my list numbered close to 25.

It doesn't have to be someone famous. It might be your child or your next door neighbour. It could be a client or a work colleague. Maybe it's someone who has learned to play a musical instrument late in life, that can inspire you to take it up.

Maybe you have previously read an autobiography. Why not take that book back off the shelf and leave it visible so that you are continually reminded of that person. Perhaps you can download a video of your role model in action and save it to your desktop. If you are having a more challenging day, take five minutes to watch the video or just ask yourself, 'what would he/she do right now if they were me?' I have watched a video of the Hoyts hundreds of times and they never cease to inspire me.

Write down the name of the people that inspire you and leave it visible. Surround yourself with them on a daily basis and they'll inspire you to succeed.

29

WHAT LIES BENEATH

It is your time to realise the greatness that is in your make-up

I WOULD like to tie two completely unrelated items together for the sake of a powerful message. The first is the title of the film *What Lies Beneath*, the 2000 blockbuster starring Harrison Ford and Michelle Pfeiffer. The connection stops there. I am only stealing the title.

The second is a philosophy of four-time World Ironman Triathlon Champion, Chrissie Wellington. A few years ago, I listened with great interest to a presentation the Englishwoman gave in Trinity College, Dublin.

In the last five minutes of her 60-minute delivery, Wellington said something which has stayed with me ever since. She was at pains to query how many people are sitting at home night after night leading dormant lives but who actually have a hidden talent or ability. She was questioning just how much undiscovered talent might be out there. Wellington was well qualified to query it, for once upon a time she was that person herself.

Chrissie Wellington, who was born in Suffolk, England in 1977, only took up triathlon in her late twenties. She was almost

30 before she turned professional. Sure, she had swum to a high standard in school and, yes, she had run a marathon at age 25, but one of her main motivations in doing so, was to lose weight. By professional standards, her finishing time in her first marathon was very modest.

That evening in Trinity College, Wellington shared a story of how she had to borrow a second-hand bike from a friend for one of her first triathlons. She confessed that she enjoyed the social side of sport a lot more back then.

Soon after her debut, Wellington headed to Nepal on a work sabbatical. Whilst in the Himalayas, she mountain-biked for fun and ran in the Kathmandu valley at weekends. Two years later (2006), and despite never having kayaked before, she entered a 243km adventure race in New Zealand and finished in the runner-up spot.

Later that year, she came back to England and entered the Shropshire Olympic triathlon which subsequently qualified her for the ITU (International Triathlon Union) World Age Group Title (Amateur) Championships. Wellington ended up winning that title by more than four minutes. In her own words, she "trained really hard for that event for 10 weeks, juggling training 20 hours a week with my full-time job".

Despite having only competed in a handful of triathlons, in early 2007 Wellington decided to turn professional. Her career as a professional was actually very short (she retired in 2012). Sandwiched in between however, were an astonishing 13 Ironman victories (she was never beaten over the distance) and four world titles. She also smashed the world record in the process.

For her, a great talent was always hidden beneath. It was only when she took part in a sprint triathlon (for fun) that it began to emerge.

It begs the question. How many of us never take up sport or challenge ourselves to take the plunge in anything. Maybe this is you, or maybe there is a family member you might tell this story to. Maybe it's a close friend or that person living next door. Of course, everyone is entitled to do as they wish, but I am sure Wellington is glad she left her comfort zones.

In so many ways, it's the decision to change something in our lives that is often the hardest part. The reward for doing so however, can be so great.

It's like the line from the song *Fix You* by Coldplay:

'If you never try, you'll never know.'

30

THE REWARD GAME

**Treat yourself along the way, as part of
changing your habits for the better**

SOMETIMES I buy a book, but it could be a year before I get around to actually reading it. That's not unusual for me. Normally I have a number of interesting books on tap, with an aim to read between 10-15 books a year.

One book I had left aside for a long time was called *The Power of Habit* written by *New York Times* reporter, Charles Duhigg. It explains the theory of why habits exist and even more importantly, how they can be changed.

In the early part of the book, he narrates the tale of Claude C. Hopkins, an advertising genius of the early 20th century. Hopkins had a track record of delivering pioneering sales successes with products such as Palmolive Soap, Quaker Oats and Good-Year Tyres. Hopkins was largely responsible in later years for encouraging Americans into a regular tooth-brushing habit which hadn't really existed previously. His secret was the realisation that people love to be rewarded for new behaviours. The reward with toothpaste, was the refreshing taste it left as well as a promised enhanced smile.

Through other examples in the book, Duhigg came to the conclusion that people are far more likely to sustain a habit when a reward is attached. A less than positive example he used was of a parent who – on an almost daily basis – ate small portions of their child's dinner despite not being hungry. Whilst the adult's goal was never to eat the food, it became a habit because of the taste it provided, i.e. the reward. By applying the opposite, if you are struggling to adopt a desired habit, why not attach a reward? You have probably used this strategy with your children. Why not benefit from it yourself?

I will use exercise as an example here, but it applies equally to any goal. Many people have a goal to adopt a healthy exercise regime. If that's you struggling to make it a permanent habit, why not reward yourself for doing so? Those who exercise regularly know that the ultimate reward is the endorphin release it gives us and obviously the knock-on health benefits. But not everyone sees this, at least in the initial stages. Early into a new habit-forming period, the whole undertaking can be quite hard and overwhelming. Newbies, in fact, almost certainly will severely dislike this new activity at first. Often they give up on doing something really positive in their lives, just before it clicks into becoming a new habit.

I would urge you to consider rewarding yourself for this new positive behaviour from the start, so that you will persist with it long enough to become a habit. By offering a reward in the early stages of this new behaviour, you are far more likely to keep the routine going.

Rather than associate a feeling of exhaustion or nausea (which you might feel in the first few weeks), focus on a reward. This might be a delicious smoothie afterwards, or a tasty treat at elevenses (which will be well-earned). Or you might commit to doing physical exercise three times a week in return for a larger reward such as a nice meal in a nice restaurant or a weekend trip to the cinema. If you follow through with three months' activity, a weekend away might encourage you to stay on track in the early stages.

By focusing on the reward at the end – whether that's on the day itself or at some near point in the future – if that reward means enough to you, it may be the key to permanent change.

Pretty soon, the morning treat or weekend away will be unnecessary, because the behaviour will now be routine. Ironically, it is just a crutch until you start feeling the other benefits, which soon after, will have you feeling great.

And isn't that the greatest reward of all.

31

WINNING TEAM

**Who you surround yourself with is
more important than you think.**

I LIKE to study human behaviour. You can learn so much about people from observation alone. Once, based on a brief non-verbal interaction that we shared, I formed a warm opinion of two septuagenarians. I was driving down the main street of my hometown one day, when I gestured from behind the wheel to the two pedestrians to cross in front of me.

As they crossed, the elderly man gave me a hearty wave. A warm smile from this man lit something inside me. His influence was immediate and even as he passed, I felt my mood improving.

Then something even more interesting happened. The lady who was with him, unaware of his gesture because she was ahead of him, repeated almost identically what he had done by waving and smiling too. As they reached the sanctuary of the footpath, both stopped, turned in my direction and gave me a further big happy wave. The synchronisation in their movements would have rivalled ice-skating duo Torvill and Dean. Two people I didn't even know had brightened up my day.

It led me to think of the influence other people have on our lives. Even as we try to achieve our goals, I believe we must surround ourselves with great people. I don't believe anybody has ever achieved anything without assistance – or influence in some capacity – from someone else.

I have also long since learned that we are the sum of the average five or six people whom we spend the most time with. Perhaps this is a prime example. That elderly couple seemed to bring out the best in each other.

I believe there are many kinds of people we can surround ourselves with to achieve our goals.

Here are some examples.

We surround ourselves with people who have a skill-set to teach us something new, such as a coach, a mentor or a manager.

Others whom we might enlist are those who motivate us or hold us accountable (a work colleague or a friend).

Finally (and I have seen great empowerment in this final one to help me achieve my goals), we can surround ourselves with people who inspire us into a state of heightened energy such as a role model or an Olympian.

We don't have to meet or speak to someone to surround ourselves with their influence. We can observe from a distance, read a book, see a TV programme or be moved or educated from hearing of their success or a story of endeavour.

Often I see people influenced by those who might not necessarily have the correct skill-set to match. Make sure that you seek counsel or take influence from the right people. When preparing for something big or if you are immersed in any kind of challenging goal, it can be easy to be persuaded by everyone at the coffee table. Choose and filter information wisely and from the right sources. Yes, someone might have value in one area but be careful not to assume that everything they say is correct. Too many opinions can sometimes spoil your goal.

It is also important that we surround ourselves with positive people. I am not suggesting that we eliminate less than positive people from our lives, but it doesn't mean you have to allow negativity to filter into your own psyche and hold you back. I'm talking about people who are close to you or those you might have strong relationships with. The trick with such people is to hear their opinions, but not to heed them. This will ensure you are respecting them but also getting the most out of that relationship for you too.

As the septuagenarians disappeared up the street, I saw a bus pass in the opposite direction. I was reminded of a philosophy from Jim Collins's book, *Good To Great*. In it he speaks about the need to get the right people on your bus, the wrong people off your bus and critically to make sure that the people on your bus are sitting in the right seats.

32

UNDERSELL AND OVER-PERFORM

Often it's good to keep your ultimate vision under wraps

WHETHER it's personal, business or even in sports, I have a strategy with my goals – undersell and over-perform.

When I came up with the notion of running 32 marathons in 32 consecutive days, I knew I wasn't nearly fit enough. I had an honest conversation with myself, where I accepted that I was only at a 5 on the fitness ladder. If I wanted to run a marathon every day for more than a month, I felt I had to reach 10.

Part of my strategy was to keep what I'd just assessed and my ultimate goal, a secret. If I revealed to others where my fitness levels were, they wouldn't have taken me seriously.

And rightly so.

I decided I had to get to 8 on the fitness ladder before contemplating making any public pronouncements on the challenge. I surmised if I couldn't get to 8, I had no chance of reaching 10.

There are times when I see people try to reach 10 straight from 5. That's where people target something that's not realistic for the stage they are at. For instance, take someone with a goal to lose an over-ambitious amount of weight. They announce their decision to lose that three or four stone – a level beyond realistic at that time. When they fail to hit the target they have broadcast to their family and friends, their confidence gets knocked and that can result in a situation where they end up putting on even more weight.

I would urge you to counter this, as I do myself, by inching ever closer to your ultimate ambition. Serve your interim apprenticeships first and by all means keep the bigger goal as a target. But consider keeping it within your own confines while you learn how to grow into the challenge you face.

I would recommend the individual seeking the weight loss should have gone for a more modest announcement – a 14lbs reduction initially. It might ultimately become 42lbs (three stone) but get to 14lbs (one stone in weight) first.

Before I set out on the 32 marathons road, I had completed two Ironman triathlons – 2.4-mile swim, 112-mile cycle and 26.2-mile run. That got me to the 5 that I mentioned earlier.

To tick the 8 box, I decided to train for one year for a double-iron distance triathlon. That's a 4.8-mile swim, a 224-mile cycle and a 52.4-mile run. I felt that if I couldn't do that, then it was unlikely I could run 32 marathons in 32 days.

I spent a year preparing for that double-iron attempt. When I crossed that finish line, both my legs and my brain were filled with a heightened confidence.

Still, though, I knew I had another year's apprenticeship to serve which – if executed – would mean I had arrived at 10 in terms of fitness. That involved more running than I had ever done before. (Ken Whitelaw, who did the 32 marathons with me, and I peaked at just over 110 miles a week in training.)

After that, I would just need Lady Luck to smile too. We all need some of that from time to time.

My approach is the same in business where I set lofty goals – undertake some apprenticeships first. Then, when my CV has more weight attached, I can announce further intentions.

If I do this, then I will have secured more credibility, heightened belief and more respect from others too.

In recent times, I've begun to target working more in America.

Some 18 months before, I was invited out to the east coast of the United States for a series of four speaking engagements over as many days.

This was due to work I had done with an American pharmaceutical company in Ireland who had recommended me to their US colleagues.

Following that apprenticeship, I'm happy to say publicly that my aim is to do a lot more speaking at conferences in the US. If I had announced two years ago that I was going to do X number of talks without testing my content on an American audience, I would not have known if I had a true value that travelled across the Atlantic. That would be the same as someone announcing they are about to run a marathon without ever having previously tested themselves to any significant running degree.

What is your equivalent?

If you're a Grade One pianist with ambitions to reach Grade Six, then why not get to *Two* and *Three* first. Then when you do, share your *Six* ambition. The skills you will learn in getting to Three will fill you with confidence and add credibility to your ultimate vision.

It's the same if you're trying to win a national title. Maybe win a provincial title first. A friend of mine applied this strategy back in 2012 with a team he was managing. At first he and his team announced a goal to win a provincial football title. Then when they had that done, they announced their ultimate ambition was to win a national football title. A few months later (April 2012) they won that final and the All-Ireland dream was realised.

His strategy was to undersell and to over-perform.

Can you see the value?

◆　　　◆　　　◆

Before you announce you're going to write a best-seller, maybe write a first draft of your book and show it to a publisher. Perhaps it means breaking 3:30 for the marathon before you announce your ambition is actually to run a sub-three. Maybe it's getting to assistant manager before telling the world you will soon be a manager; or targeting market A with a new product before targeting B and C.

I recall someone telling me they would soon be opening a chain of shops in a particular industry. At the time they had one.

Now they have none.

I believe they got carried away, lost focus and as a consequence didn't manage what they already had.

Undersell and over-perform.

It's a better route to go.

33

COMMITMENT IS...

Can you keep going long after the mood of initially taking on something has left you?

I HAD the pleasure of getting to know a man not too long ago. He was someone in his late thirties who had a big sporting ambition on his horizon. On top of that he was trying to raise a large sum of money for charity.

In the course of our conversation, we touched on the power of quotations and how they can inspire us. He shared one of his personal favourites – I'll reveal it on the next page – and it has been engrained in my memory bank ever since.

It got me thinking about the power of quotes and as to how we can be influenced by them.

◆　　◆　　◆

I have three special ones which I use often in my daily life. The first one is:

"Pain is temporary, success is forever."

I recall seeing that quote on a piece of cardboard held up by a supporting spectator at a sporting event I was participating in several years ago. It reminded me of the sacrifices I had made in terms of training to get there, with the possibility of finishing an Ironman triathlon.

It also told me that the discomfort I was experiencing at that exact moment was temporary. If I kept going forward it would eventually be worth it. Fortunately I finished that event and the medal has proudly adorned my home ever since.

The second quotation that influences me came from Michael Jordan, the American basketball icon who once admitted:

> *"I've missed more than 9,000 shots in my career. I've lost almost 300 games. Twenty-six times I've been trusted to take the game-winning shot and missed. I've failed over and over and over again in my life – and that is why I succeed."*

What I took from that is that we shouldn't be afraid to fail. In making mistakes we can learn and grow. It is a powerful message to inspire us, if things aren't going our way.

My third quotation is one that drives me because it has such truth in it:

> *"Enthusiasm is more important than innate ability because the single most important element in developing an expertise is the willingness to practise."*

That quotation comes from American author, Gretchen Rubin in her book, *The Happiness Project*. It highlights the value of bringing unrelenting enthusiasm to our ambitions as well as a willingness to practise. Just doing something often, can help us climb the highest peaks and reach the furthermost finishing lines.

And now back to the man in the opening paragraph. When I met him he was addressing an audience. He was asking them to help him with two big goals – the first was to run a great distance and the second to raise a considerable sum for charity.

He wanted their help to logistically piece together his big ambition and was seeking therefore, a big commitment from them. It would require sacrifice, effort and significant amounts of time. He wanted to ensure they came into it with their eyes open.

So often we are motivated to begin a journey. It's the commitment levels we bring, which usually determines how far we get. Like me, I think he got them on side when he said this:

"Commitment is doing what you said you would do, long after the mood you said it in has left you."

I really love that quote.

It is often easy to begin a journey to a goal. It is easy to be motivated after being inspired. If a goal is any way challenging however, then at some stage our commitment levels will be tested and usually at a time when our mood does not match our initial enthusiasm.

Often I need to memorise quotes, but not on this occasion. It resonated immediately.

We can all be motivated or inspired to dream or to do. But talk is cheap.

Commitment.

That's what separates the doers from the dreamers.

34

SECRET WEAPON

Dedicating extra time to a goal is a sure way of achieving it

AFTER three years of study, I am at the time of writing within touching distance of a long-held college ambition.

It's been a big challenge to go back studying in my forties. I've had to adjust my lifestyle to integrate more than two dozen assignments and regular attendance blocks at lectures into my working schedule.

Thus far, although I'm hesitant to put this in writing until I actually get to the finish-line, my results have been what I'd hoped for. And like the rest of my peers, I am quite proud of what's been achieved since I signed up for the course.

If the 17-year-old me could have looked 30 years into the future and seen the qualification I'm endeavouring to secure (an MBA), he would have thought it was a fairytale that could never be realised.

Back then (1985) my academic marks were lower than the readings on an outdoor thermostat during an Irish winter. My final secondary-school exams saw me secure the very minimum grades required to pass.

That was at a time when school and I were not best friends.

I am older now, and wiser too, both in understanding strategy and capability. These have led me to find an alternative route to securing higher grades.

Elsewhere in the book, I have cited the author, Gretchen Ruben. The American has a 26-word nugget of success wisdom in her book, *The Happiness Project*.

Remember in it, she said: *"Enthusiasm is more important than innate ability because the single most important element in developing an expertise is the willingness to practise."*

Before signing up for that college course, I had a chat with myself. I knew that if I was to be successful, I would have to bring an unrelenting work ethic to attain the required standard. I had to ask myself was I prepared to do the following.

If one of my fellow classmates had to do one hour of study to present a standard of work so as to get a certain grade, I had to be prepared to offer, sacrifice, deliver, practise (call it what you like) three hours.

If he or she needed to do three hours, then for me it would require nine.

It meant that before I started, I committed myself to being prepared to work three times harder than anyone else to achieve the same result. That way I could achieve grades that would match or even on occasion, surpass my fellow students.

A quick caveat is important here. If you are sharing this message with a young student, I'm not saying that this is an instant route to matching the best-performing student in the class. Be careful not to suggest that. It is, however, a sure-fire way of improving yourself and climbing further up your own academic ladder. Over time, and depending on how much you want and devote to it, you can get much higher in that pursuit than you might previously have thought possible.

I recall one particular assignment of just 1,200 words I had to hand in. Some of my classmates found it challenging, others not so much. Personally, I was flummoxed by it.

As a consequence, their 10 hours was a good 30 hours of practise for me. This strategy has been my secret weapon all along. Perhaps it might be of value to you or you could share it with someone who is studying themselves. This simple principle of working harder can help us attain higher levels in all walks of life. As I have said so often, it can apply to any goal.

When I sit down to write books, I have to devote a three-to-one strategy to even come close to the standards of a writer who is naturally (or by learning) proficient in the art.

In the first year or two of my speaking career, I devoted 16 hours of research and preparation to deliver a one-hour presentation. Now through experience and improved proficiency myself, I have it down to seven or eight hours. Truth told, I could get away with less now, but that might lead to a drop in my standards and I am keen to get better, not worse.

That means I follow through on a commitment to do that number of hours. I look at other speakers and I know they are very talented at what they do. They don't need the preparation time that I do.

But I don't mind.

I recall a different academic course I had signed up for back in 2003. One particular subject baffled the entire class. So four of us got together and taught it to ourselves. That Christmas we devoted an entire weekend (c. 24 hours of study) to making sure we understood the theory, so we could present it in the upcoming exam. The fact that we came first, second, third and fourth was never lost on me. We got out of it what we had put in.

This strategy is for those of us who feel we are not as adept as others. It is for those of us who are still keen to get there and so are prepared to travel a longer journey to get to the same end destination.

It is called the 'willingness to practise, more' – those who employ it need to do three times more than the rest. If we do, we can do better than we might otherwise have thought. And attain a standard that we might have thought was, well... a fairytale.

Over the years, I've found it to be my secret weapon.

It can be yours too.

35

THE MIGHT OF WRITE

**Write your goals down and keep them visible –
it helps you hit them more often**

I ACHIEVED a major lifetime ambition in less than six months just before the new millennium. When I analysed the reasons I was successful, one strategy in particular stood out.

I wrote down my goal. Result, I achieved it.

As a consequence, I have been using it ever since.

Now, you might be thinking to yourself, I paid good money for this book. Is that the best you can offer me? Well maybe you do it already, but I was 31 years of age at the time and it was the first time I had ever written down a goal in my entire life.

If you do it already, you probably subscribe to its value and you might want to skip this chapter. For the rest, I encourage you to read on.

It may be anecdotal, and I found it hard to get specific reference, but there was an apparent study carried out on the 1979 Harvard MBA program where graduate students were asked: "Have you set clear, written goals for your future and made plans to accomplish them?" The result was that only three per cent had written goals and plans, 13 per cent had goals but they weren't in writing and 84 per cent had no goals at all. Ten years later, the same group was interviewed again and the results were interesting to say the least.

The 13 per cent of the class who had goals but did not write them down were earning twice the amount of the 84 per cent who had no goals. The three per cent who had written goals were earning – on average – 10 times as much as the other 97 per cent of the class combined.

Writing down your goals is a simple strategy to employ but it's not as easy as it seems.

I once said that to a group of 50 well-educated thirty-somethings in a room.

"What do you mean by, 'it's simple, but it's not easy'?", they asked.

I asked them two questions.

"Do you all agree we should write down your goals? And do you agree you are more likely to achieve them, if you commit them to paper?"

Yes, they acknowledged collectively.

"Well, raise your hand if you've ever written a goal in your life."

One hand went up.

You see, it is simple to write down our goals but only one or two per cent of the population do it.

Do you?

Is it a guarantee that you will achieve your goal? Well, no.

But it does increase your chances hugely.

By the way, even if you are on the journey to your goal already and you haven't written it down, you still can. It's never too late.

Want to elevate your chances of success even more?

Keep the goal visible. Carry it in your car, in your handbag, in your gym-bag or in your school bag. Have it on your office desk or in a drawer where you can see it often. It will keep you connected to it.

That's simple too, but it isn't easy either.

Good luck with writing yours.

WANT A WORLD-CLASS SPEAKER FOR YOUR CONFERENCE?

LOOKING FOR A TOP SPEAKER TO MOTIVATE AND INSPIRE YOUR TEAM?

SINCE 2010 Gerry Duffy has worked with more than 300 companies and organisations in Ireland, UK, mainland Europe and the USA and with audiences ranging from 10 to 1,000.

His particular strengths are in working with CEOs, Senior Leaders, Executive Management and High Performance Teams.

Areas of Expertise
- Goal Setting
- Leadership
- High Performing Teams
- Motivation
- Culture and Core Values
- Personal Development

For more information

www.gerryduffyacademy.com

FEEDBACK FROM INTERNATIONAL CLIENTS

MARK TREANOR (Director of ICT Operations and Customer Services at Leaseplan Information Services)
Thank you for your presentation to our team in London yesterday. I found your talk nothing short of fantastic. I loved the ease at which you translated your remarkable achievements into such a simple, practical and 'can do' approach. The concepts you presented were so easy to grasp and relate to from a personal or business perspective – the examples for each concept are as powerful as the credibility your experiences have brought to them. I hope we will use your valued input again in the future.

COLM LONG (Director, Online Sales Operations, Europe, Middle East & Africa, Facebook)
At Facebook, we pride ourselves on attracting top quality speakers from a wide range of disciplines. The perspective which they bring really helps our teams to understand and appreciate how others overcome challenges in their own careers. Gerry's talk was one of the best I have seen. His fascinating personal journey was shared in a humble and genuine way which meant that everyone in the room was able to connect with his story. He really made us think about the goals we set ourselves and he has pushed us all to rethink our limits.

KRISTEN PARR (VP General Manager, Alkermes plc, Wilmington, Ohio, USA)
We invited Gerry to visit two of our US facilities to spend time with our leadership teams and speak to our employees in a town

hall setting. All I can say is WOW!! The content and messages are delivered for the benefit of the people sitting in the room – each one taking away a personal message. You could hear a pin drop as people were so drawn into his story. He has inspired our team to raise our personal expectations in incremental ways (at work, with family, our health) to achieve all that we can be. Days later you will still be thinking about your time with him.

EITHNE BOHAN (MD Lundbeck Irl, Specialists in Psychiatry)
How do you teach your group that they can reach any goal to which they aspire? How do you instill confidence to such a level that they expect only the highest standards from themselves? One step is to give your team the gift of listening to Gerry Duffy, a regular guy who has achieved extraordinary achievements. Gerry connects at a human level. I can honestly say that he is the best motivational speaker I have ever heard.

ANTHONY DALY (Dublin Senior Hurling Manager)
'2013 will go down as Dublin hurling's finest season in 52 years. Not only did we win the National Hurling League 1B title, we also won promotion back to the top flight in April (Division 1A). Later that summer, we won the Leinster Senior Hurling title for the first time since 1961. Definitely the best decision I made in the whole year was to invite Gerry Duffy to present to the players and my backroom team in February. In my time as an inter-county manager (nine years) and as a player (12 years) I have listened to many motivational speakers. I have found that even the really good ones find it difficult to hold the attention span of a group of players who have not only worked a normal day but have also completed a hard 90-minute training session. To say that Gerry captured the room is an understatement.'

JUST WHEN YOU
THOUGHT IT WAS TIME
TO PUT THIS BOOK ON EBAY...

THE 36th STEP

Commit to speaking a new (positive) language from here

IF you are embarked on something sizeable, something that's going to test you substantially, this final strategy is a very useful ally. If you tend to speak a 'negative' language, it's possible the only person you are hurting is yourself. Having one opponent in sport, in the business marketplace or in pursuit of any goal is hard enough, without adding yourself into that mix.

In this story, I'll be brief. But please, please take this recommendation on board.

◆　◆　◆

I once heard the Irish boxing legend and Olympic champion Katie Taylor being interviewed. In that television soundbite, she was being questioned about an upcoming bout against a feisty opponent.

"Hopefully I'll get a win," Taylor replied, when speaking about her chances and hopes for the fight.

Now here is the nub of this strategy if you want to use it to achieve *your* goals... Do you honestly think this boxing juggernaut was going to climb into the ring with the word 'hopefully' clinging limply to her biceps and triceps?

Not a chance.

Taylor was just being modest, humble and perhaps respectful to her opponent. But you can be absolutely certain, she had an utterly different mind-set and language going on in her head. I don't know her, but I am certain as certain can be, that Katie Taylor doesn't do *hopefully*.

So that's Katie.

What about you?

Are you the kind that says hopefully but really *mean* hopefully. Do you use weak or soft language when outlining your ambitions? Are you guilty of using language and phrases such as, "Hopefully I'll get it done", "I'll try", or "I'm doing it but..."

And then do you buy into the true meaning of the phrase?

Only use this language to be modest, humble or respectful to your opponent; or because you have yet to get the job done. You also have permission to use it publicly when aligning with another strategy in the book – *undersell and over-perform*.

But quietly, in your mind, speak a different language. Go forward with words of true commitment to what you are planning to achieve. In your head, use phrases like "I will", "I'm going to", "When I get there, I'll", or "I'm certain we will" etc.

Muhammad Ali never said: "I hope I might be a world champion some day," did he?

Even when he was taking his first steps into the professional ranks, he had an unequivocal vision of himself.

"I am the greatest," was his mantra to everyone who wanted to hear – but most particularly to himself. Notice that he didn't say: "I hope after learning my trade for two or three years that I might be No 1."

He left nobody in doubt, especially himself.

By doing so, he already turned his ambition into a sort of future history. He created his own reality with the words he used. You can do – and be – the same. Without realising it, you are telling your physical body, what your mind has already decided is going to happen.

Practise your version of "I am", whether it is "I will", "I'm certain I'll," or "When we get there, we will." (as appropriate)

And be careful too, of eradicating woolly thinking which comes when you use words such as:

- *"Yes, I'm sitting the exam but I didn't get as much study done as I wish I had."*
- *"I'm doing the marathon, but I've only got to 19 miles in training."*
- *"We will try, but we just don't have the budget of our competitors."*

Such phrases weaken your self-perception. If you are going to do whatever it is you are going to do, then don't sabotage your chances of doing it.

Rather, commit totally.

Perhaps, imagine you are Katie Taylor getting into *your* boxing ring. No matter how well or not Taylor's training has gone, she will – by then – have a singular mindset and will be speaking a very different language. Although we cannot get an insight into her head, be sure she is saying: "I'm going to dominate this fight", or "I'm going to win."

Now that you have come to the end of the book, I encourage you to commit to practising and speaking this language from now on.

Here are some examples:

"I will start it immediately." (not tomorrow, like so many of us say so often).

"I will lose 5 lbs by... (Time and Date)."

"I am going to write it by... (Date)."

"I will pass them... with honours, (by a set time)."

"I am going to score."

"I'm certain I'll win."

When you phrase statements in this manner, you are filling your brain with a strong foundation, from which aligned action can be launched.

◆　　◆　　◆

Here is one final one example...

"If I don't succeed at first, I will keep at it until I become fluent in thinking and speaking this way."

By doing so, you will become *The Goal Getter*.